"Offering a refreshing approach, the McCluskeys capture the essence of marital sexual intimacy with a much needed emphasis on the emotional-spiritual connection so vital to couples discovering complete sexual satisfaction."

DR. CLIFFORD AND JOYCE PENNER
best-selling authors of *The Gift of Sex* and *Men and Sex*

"*When Two Become One* will challenge you to celebrate God's good gift of sex in your marriage and will help you create a deeper intimacy and connectedness with your spouse. The question & answer sections just may answer yours!"

DAVID AND CLAUDIA ARP
authors of the 10 Great Dates series
and *Love Life for Parents*

"*When Two Become One* helps couples understand sexual intimacy as an act of worship, painting a beautiful picture of the way God intended it."

AL DENSON
award-winning Christian artist/songwriter

"The McCluskeys unveil a model to assist couples in growing deeper in their love for God and one another. Enjoy this magnificent picture of marital love as commitment, action, devotion, and sacrifice."

WILLIAM R. CUTRER, M.D., OB/GYN
certified Christian sex therapist, author of *Sexual Intimacy in Marriage*,
and Gheens professor at Southern Baptist Theological Seminary

"A soon-to-be classic on sexuality within the Christian community."

DR. ROBERT MCCALL
coordinator of missionary care,
Church of God World Missions International

"With biblically informed wisdom and clinically shaped insight, the McCluskeys have crafted a sensitive, practical, and God-glorifying classic. If you read only one book on this subject, this ought to be the one!"

DR. SANDRA WILSON
author of *Released from Shame* and *Into Abba's Arms*

"Christopher and Rachel blow away the mist that has shrouded the sacrament of marriage, revealing the biblical truth that sexuality is the physical picture of a spiritual reality."

MONTE AND KAREN SWAN
authors of *Romancing Your Child's Heart* and *Hearth and Home*

"*When Two Become One* captures the true spirit of making love, affirming a woman's desire for relational intimacy and bonding, as well as encouraging passion. Couples will grow in their sense of God's delight as they enjoy his 'wedding gift.'"

DEBRA TAYLOR, M.A.
certified sex therapist and coauthor of
Secrets of Eve: Understanding the Mystery of Female Sexuality

"This is a wonderful book that speaks to the sacred heart of marital sex. I will assign couples I work with to read it together."

REV. MICHAEL SYTSMA, PH.D.
certified sex therapist and founder of
Building Intimate Marriages, Inc.

"Chris's warm, practical teaching has helped my students gain a biblical perspective on sexuality that has helped them both personally and professionally."

DR. JIM HURLEY
department chair,
Marriage and Family Therapy Program,
Reformed Theological Seminary

"Christopher and Rachel McCluskey demonstrate how sexual intimacy is not only God's plan for marriage but also a powerful means of worshiping and glorifying the Father. We'll refer to this book over and over—it's a must-read."

CLARENCE AND BRENDA SHULER
Building Lasting Relationships, Inc. (in conjunction
with FamilyLife and the Billy Graham School of Evangelism)

WHEN TWO
BECOME ONE

WHEN TWO BECOME ONE

Enhancing Sexual Intimacy in Marriage

CHRISTOPHER & RACHEL McCLUSKEY

Revell

Grand Rapids, Michigan

© 2004 by Christopher and Rachel McCluskey

Published by Fleming H. Revell
a division of Baker Book House Company
P.O. Box 6287, Grand Rapids, MI 49516-6287
www.bakerbooks.com

Printed in the United States of America

Library of Congress Cataloging-in-Publication Data
McCluskey, Christopher.
    When two become one : enhancing sexual intimacy in marriage / Christopher and Rachel McCluskey.
        p.   cm.
    Includes bibliographical references.
    ISBN 0-8007-1794-5
    1. Sex—Religious aspects—Christianity. 2. Marriage—Religious aspects—Christianity. I. McCluskey, Rachel. II. Title.
BT708.M425 2004
248.8'44—dc22   2003021137

The authors have written this book as an educational resource, not as a tool to be used for diagnosis and treatment. The information presented is in no way a substitute for consultation with a certified sex therapist, psychotherapist, or physician. Although the authors have carefully researched all sources to ensure the accuracy and completeness of the information, the publisher and authors shall have neither liability nor responsibility to any person or entity with respect to any loss, damage, or injury caused or alleged to be caused directly or indirectly by the information presented. Treatment of medical conditions, marital or emotional problems, and wellness should always be supervised by an appropriate licensed health care professional.

All case vignettes are drawn from the experiences of real clients treated by Christopher McCluskey, MSW, LCSW, FAACS, although names and significant details have been altered to protect the privacy of those involved.

This book is dedicated to Alyssa, Colin, Grace, Drew, Sarah, and any other children with whom the Lord has yet to bless us, and to your future spouses. We pray the Lord will preserve and prepare you in this most precious area of your being, that you may one day give yourselves completely and only to each other in Christian marriage.

Contents

Preface

This book is about intimacy and sexuality within Christian marriage. If you have purchased it in preparation for marriage or in the hope of healing or enhancing what you already share within marriage, you are to be commended. There is perhaps no other blessing our Lord gives that is as bonding for couples and yet has so much potential for pain and brokenness as sexuality. You are wise to do some reading and discussion with your spouse on such a powerful and volatile subject. When you do, you stand to gain immeasurably in your intimacy and oneness as a couple, as well as to avoid or turn back waves of devastation that many marriages never survive.

Since this is not an ordinary subject, this is no ordinary book. As you read these pages, you will likely find yourself uncomfortable at various points. If you and your spouse are reading aloud to each other, as we recommend strongly, you will find yourself a bit embarrassed as we address certain subjects. It is also likely that you will disagree with us at times, feeling we have taken too conservative an approach on a subject, only to find later that you feel we have been too liberal with another. Such is the nature of writing on sexuality.

We encourage you to approach this book in a prayerful attitude, asking the Lord to speak directly to you about this delicate part of his creation. We are not so much offering a definitive statement on God's gift of sexuality as we are hoping to foster a thoughtful examination to spur more dialogue in general. It is high time we wrestled through these issues more aggressively as a church, however awkward and difficult the discussion may be.

We challenge you to read this book not only for yourself and your marriage but also for your children, your church, your community, and our world. Satan has had a field day with our sexuality. Much of his success is due to the relative silence, until recently, of the church on this subject. Several prominent Christian leaders have insisted that sexuality is the *number one issue* with which the church must wrestle in the next decade. The erosion of our sexual values is destroying marriages, families, communities, and whole denominations, leaving us ill equipped to battle the destruction it is bringing on our country and the world. Reexamining God's intentions for sexuality, we must recommit ourselves to the faithful stewardship of his design in our marriages and among those with whom we have influence.

May your reading of this book be a step in that direction. May the Lord speak to you as you examine this most private and powerful gift.

Acknowledgments

It is impossible to identify all of the persons who have had an influence on something as far-reaching as one's views on sexuality. Rachel and I first wish to acknowledge the Lord our God, who has worked in each of us by his Holy Spirit and through his Word to reveal glimpses of himself and his heart for this most private area of our being. We can gratefully claim 1 Corinthians 13:12 as a life verse in this regard: "Now we see but a poor reflection as in a mirror; then we shall see face to face. Now I know in part; then I shall know fully, even as I am fully known." Oh, for that day!

Second, we must thank our parents, Walt and Jean McCluskey and Ed and Mary Ann Kravos, who gave us the rich blessing of being raised in homes where Christ was lifted up and love was lived out. You were our first experiences of God, and we are so grateful for the many ways in which you have conveyed his love to us. Thanks too for your constant prayers and encouragement as this book was being written and for the many practical ways you assisted with child care, computer assistance, and the like. It is hard to imagine our ever being able to write this book without your support.

We are thankful to Doug Rosenau. You are much more than a mentor; you are a close friend. It was you who inspired me to pursue training in sex therapy, and you have influenced me more than you will ever know. It has been a joy working alongside you in the establishment of the Institute for Sexual Wholeness and the American Board of Christian Sex Therapists, and I look forward to many more years collaborating in this desperately needy mission field.

Likewise, my other colleagues in Sexual Wholeness, Michael Sytsma and Debra Taylor, I thank you for who you are and for the ways in which the iron of your character has sharpened my own. I have the utmost respect for your clinical skills and even more for your godly hearts. Thank you for your prayers and support.

Thank you, Norm Wright, for coaching me through the composition of a book proposal, the layout of the chapters, legal issues, marketing, and the scheduling of my time to complete the project. You are a true Christian brother.

Thanks to Steve Wood for your incredible knowledge of the early fathers of the church and your research on their writings about sexuality. This would have been a very different book without you. May God richly bless you for your faithfulness.

Thank you, Debbie Allen, for your research efforts and frequent assistance with interlibrary loans of rather obscure books. I'm sure you raised a few eyebrows with some of the titles you requested! Bless you.

Thank you Gloria Riefer for weekly "kids nights" and the ways you helped with the children during the writing. Thanks too for your love and prayers.

Thanks to Mike and Maggie and the gang at La Posada. What would we have done without you on the nights we needed a break? And thanks to Kevin Mayhill for your special gift that kept me going on the roughest days of writing.

Our heartfelt thanks to all those who did proofreading of various sections, including especially Gary Collins, Gary Oliver, Bill Cutrer, Gary and Denise Nebeker, Gil and Rhonda Harryman, Clarence and Brenda Shuler, Jim Galvin, Bob McCall, and Lane Ware. Your input was invaluable.

Finally, Brian Peterson, our acquisitions editor at Revell who first approached us with this project, thanks for your guidance and assistance throughout, for your prayers and encouragement, and for your patience as we pushed back deadlines to ensure a quality result. To Mary Suggs, Sheila Ingram, John Sawyer, Twila Bennett, Ruth Waybrant, and the entire team at Revell who have seen this work through to publication, our thanks for your perseverance and true professionalism. To God be the glory.

Introduction

Rachel and I have grown accustomed to the surprised looks and nervous laughter of friends and acquaintances when they learn of my work as a Christian sex therapist. The idea strikes many as oxymoronic, as if you can be a Christian *or* a sex therapist but not a Christian sex therapist. We joke along with them and enjoy the instant reactions our revelation engenders—from immediate interest and a litany of questions to an awkward, "Oh, really?" as they look for the nearest exit. Few topics have proven to be such great conversation starters or stoppers!

Admittedly there are not many Christians practicing sex therapy, and it was not exactly my life's ambition when I went into the field of psychotherapy. I had taken only one course in human sexuality in my professional training before I felt called to it more than a decade ago. Wrongly assuming that I would only occasionally talk with people about their sex lives, I had been entirely unprepared for the level of pain and problems that would be revealed by simply asking, "How is the sexual part of your life?"

When I opened my private practice in Clearwater, Florida, my caseload became filled with persons wrestling with sexual abuse, sexual addiction, sexual aversion, sexual dysfunctions, homosexual orientation, sexual pain disorders, and any other sexual problem you can imagine. Quickly I discovered that Christians had few places to turn when they were struggling sexually, but they were hungry for answers and for healing.

My wife, Rachel, has made this journey with me, reading the books I have read, helping me process the magnitude of the problems, and wrestling through our own theology of sexuality. She has been my constant supporter, encourager, and prayer warrior. As a result of her work in this area, we have grown tremendously in the intimacy we share within our own marriage. Rachel has done extensive research into sexual norms and practices of various cultures throughout history and on the development of doctrine around sexuality within the church. Her work on covenanting and on the connection between sexuality and worship are critical themes in this book, and many of the insights are hers, although some sections are written in the first person singular for readability's sake.

This is a book about intimacy and sexuality within Christian marriage. We separate those two concepts because it is important that husbands and wives enjoy intimacy without necessarily needing to be sexual, and because (unfortunately) husbands and wives are often sexual without really being intimate. It is our conviction that God intends our sexual intimacy to be the deepest expression of the marital intimacy we share on every other plane of the relationship.

It is our hope that this book will help couples catch a bigger vision of what God intended when he designed and blessed sexual union. We believe there is a world of difference between simply having sex and truly making love. The world uses these phrases interchangeably and, indeed, the acts themselves are the same. But the spirit of *making love* is entirely different from simply *having sex*.

The first part of this book is an examination of the struggle the church has had historically in helping couples understand God's intentions for sex—the *spirit of making love*. It also examines the fallout from the sexual revolution and how the latter half of the twentieth century impacted sexuality in Christian marriage. By looking first at the origins of many of our struggles, we are better equipped to contrast a picture of health and wholeness in sexual intimacy.

The second part of the book details a schematic model called the Lovemaking Cycle. It offers a vision of lovemaking that encourages a continually deepening experience of intimacy, rather than simply offering tips on how to have better sex. Using the model, couples are able to examine each phase of their lovemaking. It provides a framework for immediate application of points in the text and for identifying problems and solutions. We suggest that couples read these sections aloud to each other to facilitate more immediate application. Each chapter concludes with several questions for couples to ponder and discuss together.

In the final part I make practical application of the model as I answer questions Christians ask most often about sex. This section illustrates how couples can apply the model to a wide range of sexual struggles. In the final chapter we issue a challenge to take these insights and not only apply them in the reader's own marriage but share them in any number of arenas in which the Lord may give him or her influence. The world desperately needs a clearer vision of God's intentions for sexuality.

We have written this book to appeal to couples at any stage of their relationship, from premarried couples and newlyweds to those married fifty years or more. We believe that sexual intimacy should be continually maturing and deepening, just as our intimacy with the Father should always be maturing and deepening. The process of being known and fully knowing (see 1 Cor. 13:12) should never stop until we leave this world and see him face to face.

Case examples throughout the book are drawn from real couples I have worked with through the years, though names and significant details have been changed to guard their privacy. These examples are used to put a face on the issues addressed and to emphasize the range of problems that can plague couples. It is likely that you will see struggles of your own in some of these vignettes.

It is our prayer that this book will accomplish at least three major objectives:

1. Readers will gain a clearer perspective on God's great gift of sexuality and create more dialogue within the church, gradually developing a far more comprehensive theology of sexuality.
2. Readers will wrestle through a greater ownership of their sexuality, enabling them to experience a continually deepening sense of intimacy and connectedness with their husband or wife.
3. This vision of sexuality will inspire readers to be more proactive in shaping the sexuality of the next generation, enabling them to finally launch a counteroffensive to the sexual revolution of the past century.

May God yet be glorified through our sexuality!

Part 1
THE BIG PICTURE

1

A Crisis in Christian Sexuality

For this reason a man will leave his father and mother and be
united to his wife, and they will become one flesh.
The man and his wife were both naked, and they felt no shame.

Genesis 2:24–25

"Honestly, sometimes I wish God never made sex in the first
place!"

As soon as the words were out of her mouth, Kim buried her
head in her hands and wept. Sam sat on the couch beside her with
a pained look on his face, obviously concerned but not knowing
what to say or do. I sat grieving with the two of them as I had
with many other couples over the previous fifteen years, aching
over how painful God's gift of sexuality had become.

This beautiful couple in their mid-twenties was sitting in my
office because they didn't know where else to go. They had expressed
skepticism that counseling would help but realized they had to do
something to keep their marriage from falling apart. Though married

for almost three years, they had yet to consummate their relationship through intercourse. Kim was unable to allow Sam to enter her.

They had tried to be patient and not force the issue, but increasingly it had become a source of tension between them. It wasn't just Sam who was frustrated; they both felt they had been robbed of something they had saved until marriage. Now they wanted to start a family but knew it was impossible because of Kim's problem.

Through their own research, they had learned that Kim's reaction was indicative of vaginismus, an involuntary spasmodic contraction of the vaginal muscles that does not allow penetration. They had tried everything the books and their OB/GYN had suggested, but the problem only seemed to worsen. By this point they both acknowledged feeling pretty hopeless.

The good news is that we were able to solve Kim and Sam's problem; there *were* answers, just as there are answers for so many other sexual struggles that couples face. The bad news is that there are so many other struggling couples.

Sometimes the problem is pain during intercourse. Sometimes it is an inability to achieve orgasm or the triggering of trauma from past sexual abuse. It may be a pornography addiction, an affair, or conflict over a specific sex act, the frequency of relations, or differing desires. It may be infertility or repeat miscarriages. Sometimes it is as simple as premature ejaculation or a general feeling that sex is wrong or dirty; other times it is as complex as homosexuality or coping with sexually transmitted diseases. The point is that these are the all-too-common struggles of countless Christian couples.

> **Christians ought to be the most sexually fulfilled people on the planet.**

Rachel and I have long contended that Christians ought to be the most sexually fulfilled people on the planet. That doesn't necessarily mean the most sexually active or the most sexually varied in their practices, but simply the most sexually *fulfilled*. Our God is the creator of sex and, like all things he created, he pronounced it good. He affirms its enjoyment within marriage, instructing Adam and Eve to consummate their relationship *before* the fall.[1] He celebrates it in the Song of Songs, instructs us to come together frequently,[2] and pronounces the marriage bed pure and undefiled.[3] Clearly God affirms sexuality within marriage! Fostering a healthy sex life is like pouring superglue all over your relationship.

Scripture is also filled with admonitions to avoid sexual sin. These passages are very specific, often listing numerous acts that are detestable and an abomination to the Lord. We are clearly told that those who practice such things will not inherit the kingdom.[4] We are told to flee from sexual immorality[5] and to make no provision for it.[6] We are instructed to drink the water of sexual fulfillment from the well of our own marriage[7] and not to adulterate it by looking at another person with lust in our heart.[8]

So God is either glorified or blasphemed by our sexuality. It can cement a relationship together or blow it apart. Very few things have so much potential for tremendous good or unspeakable evil. Studies consistently cite sex as one of the top reasons for marital conflict and divorce. Wisdom demands that we carefully examine anything with that kind of power.

An Easy Slide into Sexual Sin

There is no denying that our sexuality is one of the strongest drives we have, and throughout history it has been one of the main areas in which God's people have struggled and failed.

However, in addition to the struggles that are common to all generations, we in the twenty-first century contend with sexual temptations that no previous culture has ever had to face. Media and the sexual revolution have wreaked havoc on the church and on her call to preserve God's gift of sexual fulfillment within Christian marriage.

Certainly there have always been impassioned invitations to enjoy the forbidden fruit of sex outside of marriage. Prostitution is called the world's oldest profession, and many cultures throughout history have had deplorable sexual values and practices. However, until the invention of photography and then of films, television, VCRs/DVDs, cable channels, and the Internet, no culture was ever daily bombarded with the graphic presentations of sexuality the way we are. Sexual images, complete with perfect lighting, background music, and models' bodies, are constantly available to us. In past generations we couldn't have seen anything close to what we see now even if we were voyeurs peeping in people's windows.

> **We in the twenty-first century contend with sexual temptations that no previous culture has ever had to face.**

Think about it. Through archeological digs and history museums, we know that sexuality has always been portrayed in art. We find nudity and depictions of sex acts on pottery, in decorative carvings on walls, in paintings, wood and clay sculptures, tapestries, and statuary. We find it in ancient writings, songs, and theatrical plays. We read of infidelity, rape, and homosexuality even throughout the Bible. But in those cultures, for a person with godly values to stray from viewing inanimate portrayals of sex in art forms to actually engaging in sinful behaviors was a fairly big fall.

Not so today. We have become the proverbial frog in the pot, so used to daily portrayals of live-action sexuality that we fail to appreciate how desensitized we have become. We have been raised on a slippery slope of magazine covers at the checkout counter, movie ads on television, daytime soap operas, romance novels, explicit music lyrics, news stories about our president's sexual practices, bikinis and fashions that leave little to the imagination, teen flicks with lots of skin, values-free sex education, and sexual humor during the family hour on TV. When we combine these with the more explicit material available in R- and NC-17–rated movies, soft-core and hard-core porn, and illicit sites on the Internet, it is easy to see why many Christians simply slide, rather than suddenly fall, into sexual sin. They have been moving in that direction for much of their lives without even realizing it.

> **We want to encourage the church with a clearer vision of God's plan for sexual union and help her respond more effectively to the state of sexuality in Christian marriage.**

This relatively new phenomenon of being exposed to hundreds of thousands of portrayals of sexuality has had another devastating effect besides the enticement to sin: *It has caused us to develop a host of unrealistic expectations of what sex should be like and these faulty expectations are destroying countless marriages.* We have unwittingly programmed ourselves to expect sex to be like what we've seen in the movies, and, when it doesn't measure up, it becomes one of the primary sources of conflict for couples. Just as the ultrathin models in magazines and movies have caused millions of women to struggle with their body image, graphic portrayals of sexuality have left millions of couples dissatisfied with their sex life because of unrealistic expectations and false information.

Our heart is never to criticize the church, for she is the bride of Christ, and we must never tear her down. Instead, our desire is to build her up and challenge her to pursue an ever-greater degree of holiness and righteousness as she awaits the return of her Groom. We want to encourage the church with a clearer vision of God's plan for sexual union and help her respond more effectively to the state of sexuality in Christian marriage.

The Church's Role

There is no question that Christians have struggled to address the rapidly changing sexual values in our culture. To a large degree we have remained silent because sex is such a private matter and so awkward to address publicly. It is certainly not the easiest subject to preach on from the pulpit. When we have addressed it, we have often focused only on what *not* to do, thus appearing prudish, old-fashioned, and judgmental and causing the world to portray us as simply not wanting anyone to have fun. Overall we have had an extremely difficult time clarifying what we *are* supposed to do with this incredible gift.

Our awkwardness and relative silence are reasons the sexual revolution was able to establish such a foothold so rapidly. When Alfred Kinsey launched the revolution in 1948 with the publication of *Sexual Behavior in the Human Male,* it hit like an atomic bomb, partly because no one else was talking openly about sex. The church, and even the scientific community, didn't know how to respond. It was not until 1981 that many of Kinsey's research methods were shown to have been fraudulent and that his claims about childhood sexuality were based on the criminal sexual abuse of more than three hundred infants and children.[9] By that point we had experienced more than thirty years of Kinsey's influence, and it had forever changed our world.

As the sexual revolution preached its gospel of free love and sex without consequences, the church of the twentieth century evangelized the masses and brought the lost into the body. This is her primary calling and is greatly to her credit. Unfortunately, since she didn't openly talk to these new converts about sex, in spite of their questions and struggles, they took their cues from the culture instead. We began to see a number of sexual practices and beliefs crop up in the church for which we had no theological underpinnings. We didn't know why we believed what we were beginning to believe, and that is always dangerous for the church.

> **We have somehow failed to redeem and sanctify sex.**

As we ushered the lost, with all of their sexual brokenness—their trauma, perversions, beliefs, and practices—into the church, we admonished them to put away their evil ways but struggled to give them a vision of God's original plan for sexual intimacy. We have somehow failed to redeem and sanctify sex. It has seemed too worldly, too fleshly; we haven't been sure what to do with it. Most seminary degrees do not require even a single course in it. Many of our premarital counseling programs barely touch on the subject. Intellectually we know it is part of God's design and is therefore good, but practically speaking we have largely left couples to fumble around with it, trying to figure out how it works and God's original plan for it. As a result, couples have looked back to the culture for the instruction the church has failed to give.

Perhaps this is nowhere more evident than in the issue of birth control. Few Christians realize that until at least the 1930s the Catholic church and the Protestant church were absolutely united in their stand against artificial means of contraception.[10] In spite of numerous forms being in use since the time of the ancient Egyptians, there is not a single church father, including the leaders of the Reformation and the Great Awakening, who supported contraception in any form.[11] When the issue began to be debated in America, there were outcries from all denominations and even from major newspapers, including the *Washington Post* and the *New York Times*.[12] The president of the United States denounced it publicly,[13] as did many prominent thinkers and writers of the day (including Sigmund Freud! [14]). Every state in the United States had laws prohibiting it. Not until 1965 did the Supreme Court rule that contraception is a constitutional right (while clarifying that it is a right *extended only to married couples*).[15]

Of course today most Protestants teach that many forms of contraception are acceptable and are even to be encouraged. It is rarely even considered much of a debate. But for the most part, we have not done the hard work of developing a sound theology for *why* we believe that—we simply believe it. It makes sense to us, just as it did to the culture. We didn't arrive at that conclusion by looking to the church's teaching; we gained it from the culture.

Our purpose in pointing this out is not to debate the merits of artificial contraception—that would be another book. We are simply using contraception to illustrate how dramatically our sexual practices have evolved over the period of a few decades and to emphasize that this evolution has largely been a by-product of our relative lack of a well-developed theology of sex.

In the case of contraception, after Planned Parenthood succeeded in having it legalized, people entered the church who had been practicing contraception before their conversion, and they simply continued to do so. Then apparently other converts learned that these members, who seemed like good upstanding Christians, practiced birth control and began to feel comfortable doing so as well. The culture was heavily promoting it, it has obvious benefits for couples, and since the church was not talking openly about sex and making a clear argument against it, contraception became common practice.

This pattern of beliefs and practices evolving over the past few decades with little theological debate can also be seen in our views on controversial issues such as masturbation and oral sex. Every time I speak on sexuality, I get questions about these two issues—and people usually have strongly held opinions on both—but they're often not sure *why* they believe whatever they believe. Their positions are argued more out of feeling than from belief.

This same pattern might even have continued with larger issues such as homosexuality and abortion—two other agendas heavily promoted by Planned Parenthood and others—but many within the church have mounted a counteroffensive on these issues and are studying and debating them more openly. We are at least beginning to clarify the theological underpinnings for why we believe whatever we believe about sex. We cannot

> **We often don't know what we truly believe or why we believe it.**

simply allow whatever we *feel* is right or wrong to substitute for what we *believe,* based on sound theology. Our feelings are too easily influenced by the culture. If we fail to wrestle through a sound theology, we get beliefs and practices by default rather than from conviction, creating a terribly weak foundation on which to stand.

Reclaiming God's Gift

If Satan had his way, he would take everything God created for good and make it his. In ancient Egypt he claimed many of the things in God's creation and persuaded the people to worship him through them—the sun, the Nile River, cows, frogs, even the crops of the field. Through Moses, God reclaimed his creation.

The plague of darkness took back the sun and showed that it did not belong to the sun god Ra. Changing the Nile to blood showed that it belonged to our God and not the Nile god Hopi. The plague of frogs took them back from the goddess Heqt. The plague of locusts conquered Osiris, god of vegetation.

In the twentieth century, Satan claimed sex as his. Through his "prophets" Margaret Sanger, Alfred Kinsey, Hugh Hefner, Larry Flynt, and others, he has persuaded our culture to worship sex. In *The Pivot of Civilization,* Margaret Sanger (founder of Planned Parenthood) wrote, "Through sex, mankind may attain the great spiritual illumination which will transform the world, which will light up the only path to an earthly paradise."[16]

The church must take back sex and claim the truth that it belongs to God and it is good—but only when practiced within his guidelines. This is accomplished in many ways, but most powerfully in the marital bedroom when, under the blessing of the Holy Spirit, husband and wife join themselves and the two become one flesh. Our union as husband and wife bears testimony in the heavenlies to the promised consummation of Jesus Christ and his bride, the church.

We strongly believe there is a need for visionaries, missionaries, and warriors in this culture who can address sexuality and say, "This is our God's turf! This is *not* the enemy's turf. We will no longer be silent while the culture seeps into the church. We will no longer watch passively as our couples struggle in ignorance and brokenness. We are reclaiming sex!"

God has answers. He has a plan for this gift, and it is incredibly good. We as a church must redeem and sanctify our view of sex. If we do, it can be the cornerstone of a new evangelization—the world is crying out for real answers. If we fail, it will likely be our undoing. The homosexual issue alone is already unraveling entire denominations. We simply must do a better job of discerning God's plan for sex.

Questions for Couples

- In what ways has the media and Western culture impacted your view of sexuality?

- In what areas are you most easily tempted by the culture's presentation of sexuality?

- What faulty expectations have you unknowingly brought into the marital bedroom?

- In what ways has sex become a point of contention between you and your spouse?

2

The Difficulty
of Talking Openly

Of the delights of this world, man cares most for sexual intercourse,
yet he has left it out of his heaven.

Mark Twain

Richard and Adrienne sat tensely in my office, a strained look
on their faces. It was their first appointment and, in their telephone
intake, they had simply said they needed to see me about a problem
in their sexual relationship. I opened the session in prayer and tried
to set a comfortable tone, letting them know this was a safe place
and that they could talk about anything without fear of judgment
or of shocking me. I then asked about their primary concern.

After a long silence, Adrienne shifted her gaze to a corner of
the room and began. "It's really hard to put it into words. I can't
even believe we're sitting here talking about this. We were both
raised in families that *never* talked about . . . you know, sex and
all. It just wasn't done. And we have never really talked about it
with each other—we just kind of 'do it.' But it's not working well
and we don't know what to do."

I again offered reassurance and commented that many parents never talk about sex with their children, making it difficult later for the adult children to discuss problems when they arise.

After another long pause, Adrienne continued. "Well, we've been married for eight years, and we have a pretty good marriage in most respects. We love each other, and we've been blessed with two beautiful children. Rick is a good provider and a great daddy. In most ways we're really happy. We probably shouldn't even be complaining about anything—it's not like life has to be perfect or anything . . ." She tried to look at Richard, but he just shifted nervously in his chair.

I affirmed them for having such a healthy marriage and for being willing to take steps to make it even better. It was a safe bet that neither was embroiled in an affair and that they were at least able to have intercourse since they had two children, but something was obviously troubling them greatly.

"It's just that . . . that when we, you know, do it or whatever, we never seem to be able to . . . I mean, I can never, you know . . ."

I have had countless conversations like this with couples who often take half the session or more before they can clearly explain their problem. In the case of Richard and Adrienne, their concern was that Adrienne had never been able to achieve climax. She enjoyed being close with Richard and having him inside her, but she was fairly certain she had never experienced an orgasm. (As a general rule, if a person isn't sure, it's pretty certain the person has not.)

Adrienne felt there must be something wrong with her, that she was frigid. And Richard felt that he must not be a good lover or he would be able to give his wife this pleasure. They had both gotten to the point of avoiding sex for the most part or just "getting it over with" so Richard could have some release. They were feeling more and more distant from each other in their lovemaking—a time in which God intends couples to be *most* aware of their oneness.

This case, and thousands more like it, illustrates the difficulty of talking openly about sex. Any parent who has talked with his or her children about it knows how awkward the language can be. Any pastor who has preached on it will attest to the difficulty of doing so. If couples, and we as a church, are going to reclaim sexuality, the first hurdle we must overcome is the difficulty of talking clearly and openly about it. When we are unable to use specific language, it is next to impossible to have a meaningful dialogue on any subject.

> **If we are going to reclaim sexuality, the first hurdle we must overcome is the difficulty of talking clearly and openly about it.**

There is good reason for our difficulty in discussing sex. It is the most private of matters and is not supposed to be discussed as openly and carelessly as it is in our culture. There are very few truly appropriate settings for addressing sexuality. Having young children present should prevent it from being discussed in most settings. Having mixed company, even married persons, should make such discussions somewhat awkward and uncomfortable. The privacy and sacredness of sex account for that. There is probably no perfect setting. Regardless, we must talk about it.

Holy Ground

Several years ago I was speaking at a couples retreat; Rachel was in attendance. She was in the back of the room praying for me as she often does. Before I began, I knelt down to untie and take off my shoes. After the morning session Rachel came up with a look of amazement on her face and asked, "Why did you take off your shoes?"

I replied, "Well, honey, it's a retreat—it's casual, comfortable . . ."

She said, "My prayer for you was that the ground you were standing on would be holy ground and that the words the Lord had for us would flow up through the soles of your feet and out of your mouth."

Obviously, I spoke the rest of the day in my stocking feet! And now, whenever I speak on sexuality, I do so in my stocking feet as a testimony that we are on holy ground. This is precious turf and it is very near to the heart of God. Just as we are not to take the name of the Lord in vain, we are not to speak of the sacred things of God in a careless or vain manner. We are to show proper respect for sex by the way in which we refer to it.

My experience, however, is that people do not struggle with talking openly about sex because it is so sacred and holy. They struggle because it seems so fleshly and carnal. In fact I have found that many Christians wish they didn't know God could see them making love. They view sex as some kind of fleshly indulgence from which God must turn his head. I have worked with many whose sex lives were tainted with the use of pornography or fantasy about other people because they had so disconnected sex from the rest of their walk with the Father. They were simply following the world's advice about how to spice things up.

On the other extreme, I have found many couples responding to this discomfort by simply practicing "lights out, under the covers, missionary position, no talking" sex—as if sex is a necessary evil that should be completed with as little revelry as possible. There is certainly nothing wrong with having the lights out or not wanting to vary positions, but for Christians to strip sexuality of its passion and excitement is a tragedy. The same God who commands us to have festivals and celebrations with rich foods and fine wines encourages us to drink deeply and to eat our fill in the marital bedroom.[1] Sexual union is to be a celebration of our oneness!

Poetically speaking, when God looks over the portals of heaven into a healthy Christian marital bedroom, he claps his hands in approval and exclaims, "*Yes!* Did I design that right or what? Do you experience anything else like that? *I* did that. I, God, created you to work that way, to communicate with your bodies what your words cannot—of your oneness with this other person who is, in fact, half of you. And I am with you right in the midst of it! We are 'a cord of three strands not easily broken.'"[2]

Intimate Communication

Sexual union is first and foremost a means of communication. We communicate powerful messages to each other and to the Lord when we join ourselves sexually. It is our most intimate form of communication, enabling us to say things about our spiritual oneness that words cannot.

> **We communicate powerful messages to each other and to the Lord when we join ourselves sexually.**

The word *intercourse* conveys this notion of communication. It is not an exclusively sexual term but simply means "to have an exchange or a communing between persons." Couples must ensure that the messages of their *verbal* intercourse and their *relational* intercourse line up with the messages of their *sexual* intercourse. If they are communicating love throughout the day in the ways they serve, honor, and cherish each other, then the joining of their bodies in lovemaking bears testimony to that love. If, however, they are communicating anger, hatred, criticism, neglect, or disdain, the statement of their sexual union becomes a lie. With their bodies they are saying, "I love you so much that I want to have every part of you and to give you every part of me"; but they have communicated something entirely different throughout the day.

Various Scriptures referring to God communing with his people can be literally translated as God having intercourse with his people—not *sexual* intercourse naturally but *spiritual* intercourse, a spiritual "knowing." That is why, when we stray from our relationship with God, he says we have played the harlot or become an adulteress. God frequently uses sexual metaphors when he speaks of the intimacy he desires with his bride, the church (more on this in chapter 3).

> **We have four basic "languages" from which to draw when talking about sex, and none of them is ideal.**

In addition to our misunderstanding of God's view of sex, there is another factor that accounts for our discomfort with talking openly about it. The language we have to draw on is fairly stunted and limiting. It has been suggested that we have four basic "languages" when talking about sex, and none of them is ideal. The first is *clinical language*. This is mostly what we will use throughout this book. Clinical language consists of the anatomical and medical terms for body parts and acts. We will be clear and specific in this book. We will not dishonor sexuality by referring to it so cryptically that you are not sure what we are talking about.

But neither will we be crass and use the second language, which is *slang*. Many times when couples try to explain to me what they are struggling with, this is the language they use. It is the language they heard most from their peers growing up and it is the language of our culture. They fumble around trying to find another word for *horny* or *boobs* or *getting laid,* and they finally just toss them out there with an embarrassed look on their face. I often joke with them and say something like, "Are we allowed to say that?" It breaks the tension and allows us to move on.

Clinical language certainly does not light up a bedroom. It gets the job done in a book or in explaining sex to your children, but it does not stoke your fires. Slang is just not appropriate in almost any situation, although couples will sometimes agree to use a few words in private as their secret little ways of cueing each other. The third language we have to work with is *kiddie language*. This includes words like *wee-wee, tah-tahs, tallywacker,* and *boinking.* It makes us laugh to hear these words, but we rely on them sometimes because we don't know how else to convey what we mean.

The fourth language is even worse—*euphemisms,* like "You know," "that thing," "down there," "doing it." Euphemisms can leave things so vague that we *think* we know what our partner is referring to, but we're not sure. This is the only language Richard and Adrienne had in the vignette at the beginning of this chapter. I know of the case of a preadolescent girl who kept telling her mother that her "bottom" hurt. It was only when her mother took her to the doctor for an examination that the doctor discovered she had a urinary tract infection. The child had never been given any other language for describing that entire area of her body other than "bottom."

These are the four languages we have for discussing sex. None of them is ideal for every situation. All of them leave us wishing for a better vocabulary that wouldn't make us sound dry and clinical, dirty-minded, goofy and childish, or ignorant. Perhaps that is why Scripture often uses a fifth alternative, *poetic language*.

The Song of Songs is filled with poetic references to the Lover and the Beloved. A wide array of foods, animals, trees, and other things in nature are used to describe their bodies, their desire, and their enjoyment of each other. Gardens and towers and even images from battle are used to evoke the passion they feel toward each other. Unfortunately, this language too has its limitations, as any Bible scholar will tell you. We are not certain what all of the references are meant to describe.

Effective Communication

Language is important. I remember when Rachel and I were engaged and were at a gathering of our college friends discussing where we might live once we were married. Someone asked what kind of housing we were looking at—would we get an apartment or buy a house? Rachel responded, "No, we're thinking of buying a condom." Obviously she meant a *condo*, but everyone had a good laugh and we saw again how very important language is!

> **Talking about sex is going to make us uncomfortable, and it should.**

Even though sex is a highly private subject, we must nevertheless discuss it. No matter what language we use, talking about sex is going to make us uncomfortable, and it should. If talking about it is like talking about what we had for dinner last night, we have lost something. It has become too familiar, and we have lost some of its mystery and eroticism.

In addition to making us uncomfortable, the subject of sex will also, sadly, divide us. As we have said, it is almost certain that this book will upset many of our Christian brothers and sisters. Some will feel we have been too liberal. Others will feel we have been too conservative. Sex is a volatile subject, and people's reactions to discussions of it are often like their reactions to discussions of politics and religion. There will always be disagreements.

As we said in the introduction, one of our primary goals is simply to get the church talking more effectively about sex. If that occurs, it is okay with us if we don't always agree with each other. If you bristle at something we have written, simply ponder and pray about it. Discuss it with your spouse, trusted friends, or your pastor. But let's start a better dialogue. Satan wants us to keep this quiet. As a church, let's start talking more effectively about sex.

The other thing that talking about sex will do is make us frisky! That is also as it should be. If talking about sex doesn't get our motor going a little bit, something is wrong. If it becomes so clinical and analytical that we discuss it only with our minds and not our hearts, we are missing out. We need to come to sexuality in our child ego state, with curiosity, a spirit of adventure and abandon, fun, and play. So it should leave us a bit aroused.

Finally, addressing this topic will leave many in a great deal of pain. To talk about sexuality, even in the very positive sense of God's intentions for it, can dredge up all the pain of what it has in fact been. For many, sexual experience has not been close to what God intended. For some, this is because of poor choices they have made. In many cases, it is because of things that have been done to them.

Be aware of this as you read, and check yourself periodically. Recognize that, if this topic opens Pandora's box and begins to churn up painful memories, you needn't fear them. God will meet you in your pain. You will need to take those memories out at an appropriate time with appropriate people and begin to examine them, but God has healing available. Do not allow the enemy to lay claim to anything that God has created, including your sexuality.

I have seen many couples come through God's healing for sexual brokenness of all kinds and emerge with a marital relationship that is so different from what you normally see sitting next to you in the pews on Sunday morning that it defies explanation except to say that our God is bigger than any problem. The question is not how bad was the damage—the question is how passionate are you about seeing God's power brought to bear on it for healing? God is able to heal all our brokenness when we surrender it to him.

I have seen couples with relatively small problems that would have been quite easy to work through, but their attitude was, "We can't talk about that! We don't want to go there! There's no point in looking back!" No real healing can come with such an attitude; the issues will continue to fester under the surface and pop up in various forms throughout their years together.

I have also seen couples who were basically "dead on arrival," not sure anything could be salvaged of their damaged sexuality. But their attitude was, "If there is any good that can come out of this, we are ready to do the work. We're ready to roll up our sleeves and do what is needed, and we believe God can do what is impossible for us to do alone." And he does.

So if this brings up pain for you, embrace that pain and say, "Lord, what would you have me do with this?" Accept this as God's invitation to start talking about sex. Satan works in the dark. God works in the light. Bring sexuality out into his light.

For the couple at the beginning of this chapter, their healing began the moment they began to fumble through an open discussion about their sex lives. They later told me of sobbing in each other's arms when Adrienne finally achieved climax and said that their sense of oneness and intimacy was deeper than they had experienced since early in their marriage. God has given us sexual union to express truths that our words cannot. We must not allow embarrassment and fear to muffle those truths.

Questions for Couples

- In what ways has the awkwardness of talking about sex robbed you?

- What language do you and your spouse use for communicating about sex? Do the two of you need to expand your vocabulary?

- What messages about sex do you wish had been clearly conveyed to you while growing up? Are you sharing those messages with others now?

- Think of at least one thing you have never told your spouse about your sexuality. Are the two of you being robbed because of your silence?

3

The Spirit of the Act

There were no difference between the married state and whore-
dom, were not God willing to close his eyes to it.

Martin Luther

They waited in their car until I called their cell phone to confirm
that my previous client was gone and that I would meet them at
the rear entrance to my offices. They didn't want to risk being
seen in the lobby. Jim was pastor of a large church several hours
away that had a television ministry.

As we sat down, it occurred to me that they were one of the
most attractive couples I had ever seen. Jim was a strapping 6' 3"
with broad shoulders, a strong jaw, and a rugged, outdoorsy look.
His steely blue eyes and slight graying of the temples gave him an
air of wisdom and gentleness. When combined with his charisma,
it was easy to see why people were drawn to him. Linda had poise
and grace, an elegance seldom seen these days. Her face was lovely,
her demeanor warm and inviting, and, now into her forties, she
had retained her figure.

Linda became tearful as she relayed the reason for their call. Jim wrung his hands and was unable to look at me, pacing the room at one point when his tension became too great.

"We're here primarily out of concern for our daughter, Gina. She is fifteen and well into puberty. She's a beautiful girl and good student, loves the Lord, has lots of friends, and is fairly well adjusted in most regards. We're concerned that some things we have struggled with in our marriage may be having a negative effect on her views of men and women and sex. We don't want our struggles to mess her up, and we're afraid they are."

Linda went on to explain that for most of their marriage they had only rarely had intercourse because of Jim's extreme discomfort with nudity and sexuality. Their sex life primarily consisted of her partially disrobing and Jim cuddling and rubbing against her until he ejaculated in his shorts. This was always followed by Jim feeling very bad about himself and dirty, and Linda feeling used and confused.

Naturally Gina knew nothing of this. Jim and Linda were aware that Jim's distorted view of sex was a result of his repressive, legalistic upbringing. His parents had paired such shaming messages with sexuality that he had worked most of his life not to have any sexual thoughts at all. He had not dated anyone throughout high school and college until meeting Linda his senior year. Their courtship lasted only three months, in which time they did not so much as hold hands. It was months after their marriage before they awkwardly consummated their relationship at Linda's insistence. In public they had come a long way in their interactions, with Jim now easily placing his arm around Linda or holding her hand, even giving her a peck on the cheek. But in the privacy of their bedroom the old messages held sway.

Their daughter, Gina, had begun to show interest in boys and was paying more attention to her femininity, caring for her hair and clothes and wearing jewelry and makeup. Both Linda and Jim recognized that, as Gina was becoming a young woman, Jim was pulling away from her and having a harder and harder time connecting with her and giving her hugs or goodnight kisses. His discomfort with Gina's changing body and her newfound interest in the opposite sex was creating an awkward distance and tension. At times Gina still wanted to be Daddy's little girl, but Jim recoiled if she tried to take his hand or cuddle up to him on the couch watching TV.

What's more, Jim was beginning to monitor and challenge every interaction she had with peers, especially boys, and Gina was beginning to chafe at the scrutiny. Linda had finally confronted Jim because she sensed that the growing distance in their relationship coupled with his frequent interrogations were beginning to drive Gina away and, potentially, right into the kind of relationships Jim feared the most. Indeed, as we later discovered, that had already happened.

The church has never had an easy time with sex. We have often preached what we are not to do sexually but have seldom affirmed what we are to do. Our general policy could be summed up as "Clarify the boundaries and the rest will take care of itself." But in countless cases like Jim's, a rigid emphasis on the boundaries without affirmation of the beauty and importance of marital union

> **The spirit of making love in Christian marriage is entirely different from simply having sex.**

has resulted in throwing the baby out with the bath water. We have often failed to catch the spirit of the act, focusing only on the letter of the law.

There is a world of difference between having sex and making love. Much more than just completing the conjugal act, *making love is about enhancing a couple's experience of love on all planes*

*of their relationship and having their sexual union be the truest
expression of that love.* Jesus constantly challenged us to examine
the spirit of an act. The spirit of making love in Christian marriage, bonding spirit to spirit, soul to soul, and body to body
in three-dimensional union, is entirely different from simply
having sex. As we said in chapter 2, the goal is to communicate
with our bodies what we have communicated with our words
and our lives.

This communion through our bodies is what establishes
Christian marriage as a covenant relationship.[1] Covenants
were used a great deal in the ancient Middle East because a
covenant was far more binding than a standard contract.[2] To
establish a covenant meant that the parties bound themselves
together as *family* in a relationship that could not be broken.
There are numerous examples of this throughout Scripture.
They utilized a variety of rituals, but all covenants followed
the same basic formula. The terms were spelled out verbally
and/or in writing and then consummated (sealed) in a manner that made them binding. Often this consummation involved an offering of flesh and blood that was sacrificed and
then consumed by the parties. This is part of the reason God
established the Old Testament covenant with Israel through
the institution of the sacrificial system. It was only after the
covenant was established that God called Israel his children.
They had become family.

Kings frequently covenanted with each other by giving their
daughters—their literal flesh and blood—in marriage. (This is
why King Solomon had so many wives.) The key for us to note
is that *such a covenant was not considered sealed until the union
had been consummated through sexual intercourse*—each spouse
offering his or her body to be "consumed" by the other. That
consummation confirmed the truth of their words in the cov-

enant and meant that the two parties had become one in flesh and blood. They had become family.

This is part of the reason, when God made the new covenant, he gave us his body. "Whoever eats my flesh and drinks my blood remains in me, and I in him" (John 6:56). The offering of his body confirms the truth of his love for us, and the consuming of his flesh and blood seals our oneness with him. We become family, the children of God, brothers and sisters of each other and of Christ.

Christian marriage begins with a verbal exchange of vows, pledging to give all of ourselves to each other and to receive from the other all of who he or she is—for better or for worse. During their wedding ceremony, many couples light a unity candle to symbolize this merging of the two into one. But by covenant standards, these vows are not consummated or made valid until the groom literally gives *all of himself* and the bride *all of herself* in the act of sexual union. As the two bodies become one flesh physically, the two persons become one spiritually, bonding them forever in covenant relationship. The two become one. From that day forward, every time they make love, they are renewing the vows they made on their wedding day—giving themselves completely to each other.

What more beautiful act of worship could there be than to physically and spiritually renew our vows to love, honor, and cherish each other until death? When we do so, we give our bodies not only to each other but also to God. Every act of love is an expression of God, for God is love, and he is evidenced and glorified in our love. "No one has ever seen God; but if we love one another, God lives in us and his love is made complete in us" (1 John 4:12). God's love is made complete through our words, our attention, our service, our hugs, our kisses, and most completely in Christian marriage through our sexual union.

A Strong Connection

Satan knows of this powerful connection between sexuality and spirituality, and one of his goals has always been to get people to glorify him rather than God. So he encourages us to express something other than love through our sexuality: lust, selfishness, disobedience, lies. When these are the spirit behind sex, it is Satan who is glorified and not God. *This is the key concept we must grasp to discern the true spirit of the sex act.* When sexual union expresses love within covenant Christian marriage, God is glorified. When it expresses lust, selfishness, disobedience, or lies, Satan is glorified. Remember, we worship with our bodies: "Offer your *bodies* as living sacrifices, holy and pleasing to God—this is your *spiritual* act of worship" (Rom. 12:1). The question we must always ask is, Who is being worshiped in spirit by this physical act?

Sexuality and spirituality are intimately connected.

We can see this connection between sexuality and spirituality more clearly by examining how Satan can be glorified through sex. You will recall that the nations from which Abraham was called practiced fertility religions, and sexuality was a central part of their spirituality and worship. The Canaanites used ritual prostitution, temple orgies, and child sacrifice (the product of sexual union) in their worship ceremonies. The Egyptians and Babylonians did the same. Even Israel, while awaiting Moses' return from Mount Sinai, returned to worshiping Apis, the Egyptian bull-god of sex and power. They sacrificed, feasted on the ritual meat, and offered their bodies in sexual revelry.[3] Later, before entering the Promised Land, they engaged in ceremonial relations with the temple prostitutes of the Moabite god Baal.[4]

Even after Israel had become established and was blessed with prosperity, Satan was able to quickly lure her back into the union of ungodly sexuality and spirituality in her worship. Altars and idols were erected, even within God's holy temple, to Baal and the vile gods Molech, Ashtoreth, and Chemosh. Kings Ahaz and Manasseh even sacrificed their own sons in the fires.[5]

> **God linked sexuality and spirituality in the beginning.**

When good king Josiah came to power and the book of the Law was discovered, he called Israel back from these fertility cults and destroyed their altars and idols along with their sacred stones, high places, and Asherah poles.[6] (Scholars are uncertain about the exact nature of these, but they were central to their detestable rites. It appears that sacred stones symbolized the male testicles or possibly the entire genitalia, and an Asherah pole may have been a phallic symbol, a wooden penis used in worship.[7] A gigantic one had apparently been placed in the Holy of Holies, and there were living quarters for male shrine prostitutes within the temple!)

These examples and numerous others illustrate how closely sexuality and spirituality are tied. Satan knows that if he can hook us in this area, he can sling us around in any other area he desires. When we see him in the form of these various pagan deities, he almost always has sex as a central piece of his worship. It is the same today. He has always been there saying, "This is mine."

God knows of the connection between sexuality and spirituality. He was the one who linked them in the beginning. As soon as he created Adam and Eve and began the intimate fellowship of walking and talking with them in the Garden, his first instruction was, "Be fruitful and multiply" (Gen. 1:28 NASB). In other words, "Make love. Express your love and spiritual oneness bodily, and allow me to create more love (new life) through your love."

These are the first instructions of God's initial blessing spoken over man and woman. God, who is Love, tells us to express our love for each other in him through our sexuality. In this he is glorified.

A Sign of Surrender

We see the connection between sexuality and spirituality again when God calls Abram to be the father of a new nation. He gives him the new name *Abraham* and institutes a sign of their covenant relationship—the rite of circumcision. He tells Abraham to cut the foreskin of his penis as a mark that he is God's man, and he tells him to do the same for his whole household.

What an amazing rite! God didn't accidentally make a foreskin and say, "Oops, I didn't mean for that to be there. Just cut that off." Circumcision was practiced by many of the pagan religions of that region as a means of signifying that their life was committed to their god—it was another covenantal sign, giving one's flesh and blood to consummate one's vows. God chose to claim back that sign to mark his covenant people.[8]

God told Abraham to mark in his flesh, *in the area of his flesh where he was most likely to violate his covenant relationship,* a reminder that he was not his own. He had been set apart. His body, and especially his sexuality, was not his to use in any way he saw fit. Remember that he was still living in an entirely pagan culture of fertility worship in Canaan, not far from Sodom and Gomorrah, and he had already taken his own route to ensure descendants for himself by impregnating Hagar.

If it were with our *hands* that we were most likely to violate our covenant relationship, God might have had Abraham cut off the bit of skin between his thumb and forefinger. Circumcision was just a mark. But it was a *covenantal* mark, and the Hebrews understood this. It linked them to God as family, and it linked their sexuality with their spirituality. God determined that his followers would worship him through their sexuality, but not as the pagan gods were worshiped, not through orgies and unbridled sex acts with strangers. God would once again be worshiped and glorified in the one-flesh union of husband and wife, as it was in the beginning.

Circumcision was big for the Hebrews. They understood things about it spiritually that can easily be lost for us. Jews took great pride in their mark as God's people and spoke disparagingly of those outside the covenant as "uncircumcised Gentiles." Circumcision provided an external sign, a visible reminder of who they were as God's children. Under the new covenant, God now speaks of circumcision of the heart—it applies to all of us, men and women.[9] Lacking that external sign, however, we can easily miss what it means—that we have committed our whole being to God. No longer circumcising the flesh or offering the bodies of animals on altars of stone, we are now to circumcise our hearts and offer our *own* bodies as *living* sacrifices—daily surrendering our lives to his service. We are to present ourselves as the bride of Christ, allowing him to impregnate us by his Holy Spirit to generate new life within our being.

This is the connection Paul makes when he writes, "'For this reason a man will leave his father and mother and be united to his wife, and the two will become one flesh.' This is a profound mystery—*but I am talking about Christ and the church*" (Eph. 5:31–32, emphasis added). When husband and wife make love, their union bears testimony to the union of Christ and his church, which will ultimately be consummated in the wedding feast of the Lamb!

The Power of Sex

God knew what he was giving us in sexuality, and he knew its power. Sex is one of the most powerful forces in the universe—for good or for evil. That is why God gave us such clear guidelines for its proper use. When sex is used within God's guidelines, God is greatly glorified. When it is used outside of those guidelines, God is blasphemed.

First Corinthians 6:18–20 says:

> Flee from sexual immorality. All other sins a man commits are outside his body, but he who sins sexually sins against his own body. Do you not know that your body is a temple of the Holy Spirit, who is in you, whom you have received from God? You are not your own; you were bought at a price. Therefore honor God with your body.

God is saying that, just as he was blasphemed by the desecration of the Old Testament temple through Israel's misuse of sexuality within it, *he is blasphemed anytime we misuse our sexuality, because we are now his temple!* When we misuse our sexuality, we are glorifying Satan within the very temple of God.

God is not closing his eyes to our sexual union—he is right in the midst of it!

Note, however, that the converse is also true. When we use our sexuality in accordance with his original plan, God is *glorified* in the temple of our bodies. He resides in us by his Holy Spirit and communes with us as we become one in body, soul, and spirit. He is not closing his eyes to our union; he is right in the midst of it! God is present in Christian sexual union just as he is present in the rest of our marriage, perhaps even more so because of the covenantal nature of the act. He is glorified and manifested in the sacred act of two becoming one. It is next to impossible to tear apart a Christian marriage that celebrates in this spirit of love and intimacy.

Freedom from Guilt or Shame

We have not always guarded the truth that God is glorified through marital sexual union. Numerous heresies have arisen because of the difficulty of understanding that sex is evil in most contexts but gloriously good within marriage. Dualistic heresies have arisen that espouse an either/or perspective, characterizing spirit as all good and matter, including the body and sex, as all evil. They view evil as being tied to the body through sin and, hence, the body is to blame for evil and is evil itself. Therefore sex becomes a necessary evil to be engaged in only for the purpose of procreation or to alleviate temptation. This was the perspective held by Jim in the vignette at the beginning of this chapter.

A theology that does not celebrate sexuality as a beautiful part of God's design has often resulted in efforts to suppress or repress the sex drive. At various points in history men have castrated themselves[10] and fitted young boys with

> **We were created to glorify God in the body.**

genital cuffs.[11] Women have been forced to wear chastity belts and dress in such a manner that no part of their skin could show except their face and hands. Beautiful murals by artists such as Michelangelo were ordered to have the genitals painted over with fig leaves. Even furniture with ornately carved legs was covered up with skirts so that the curve of a wooden leg might not incite lustful emotions.

There is a critical difference between *repression* and *discipline!* It is true that the sex drive is extremely powerful and that we must exercise discipline over it so that we do not dishonor God in the body. But we must always remember that we were created to glorify God in the body. We do this by singing praises and extolling his greatness in worship and by meditating on his Word and committing our lives and our labor to his service. We do it through our time and our resources, through feasting and celebrating his goodness. And we do it through the joining of our bodies as husband and wife, made in his image, rejoicing in the delight of becoming one.

Glorifying God through the indulgence of bodily appetites may at first sound scandalous, but, as Douglas Jones notes in his article "Worshiping with Body," ". . . we have a Lord who steps in and *commands* us such things as, 'Thou shalt bestow that money for whatsoever thy soul lusteth after, for oxen, or for sheep, or for wine, or for strong drink, or for whatsoever thy soul desireth: and thou shalt eat there before the LORD thy God, and thou shalt rejoice, thou, and thine household" (Deut. 14:26).[12] This is a serious feast! And God says he is glorified through it—the Israelites were to use their *tithe* to celebrate it in his honor!

Such a feast would not be glorifying at all if it were without discipline—it would degenerate into gluttony and drunkenness. We are to embrace celebrations in the flesh while still exercising discipline. The mature Christian is to have control over his or her fleshly desires while still indulging them at proper times. "The man who fears God will avoid all extremes" (Eccles. 7:18).

If this is true of food and drink, it is also true of sex. Remember that God instructs us to drink deeply of sexual love in marriage. Using exotic foods and fine wine as metaphors for sexual enjoyment, he says, "Eat, O friends! Drink, yes, drink deeply, O beloved ones!" (Song 5:1 NKJV). The entire Song of Songs is a celebration of sexual desire and enjoyment between husband and wife. It contains several beautiful passages consisting only of the couple praising each other's body and delighting in their sexual union. Proverbs says, "Let your fountain be blessed, and rejoice with the wife of your youth. As a loving deer and a graceful doe, let her breasts satisfy you at all times; and always be enraptured [literally, *intoxicated*] with her love" (Prov. 5:18–19 NKJV). These passages are not referring to sexual union purely for the sake of procreation, nor do they indicate that God is anything but pleased with our enjoyment of marital lovemaking. They are pictures of passion being released within God's established boundary of marriage—feasting with discipline.

So God is the creator of our sexuality and he has joined it intimately to our spirituality. He is blasphemed when we misuse it but glorified when it is enjoyed within his guidelines. And he is present with us in the midst of our lovemaking. This is good news for Christians—it is freedom! When the pastoral couple at the beginning of this chapter began to grasp these truths, the impact became evident not only in their marriage but in Jim's relationship with their daughter and even in the spirit of his ministry from the pulpit. God's truth brought release from his self-imposed prison.

We are free within marriage to enjoy all of the goodness God intended when he crafted our sexuality. There is no place for guilt or shame; we can be naked and unashamed. We can, at least to some degree, return to the intimacy and innocence of the Garden as husband and wife and, in so doing, foreshadow the final consummation in heaven of our relationship with Christ. What an awesome picture of oneness with him!

Questions for Couples

- ❧ What messages have you received about sex from the church?
- ❧ How comfortable are you with the idea of God being present in your bedroom? Why?
- ❧ Are there any ways in which you may be dishonoring God in your sexuality?
- ❧ In what ways would you like to change the spirit of your current lovemaking?

4

Discovering God's Heart in Our Body

So God created man in his own image, in the image of God he created him; male and female he created them.

Genesis 1:27

"I can't help it—I just don't like him to see me naked! Is there anything wrong with being modest?"

Susan's face was flushed and her eyes wide open as she sat on the edge of her chair. Her husband, Terry, sat stiffly and solemnly beside her. Over the past several months we had made fantastic progress on Susan's recovery from sexual abuse. She was able to see it for what it was and had released herself from responsibility for it, knowing she was only a child when it occurred. She had forgiven her cousin but set appropriate boundaries with him and had wrestled through her questions about where God was in the midst of it. But she was just beginning to look at its impact on her adult sexuality.

"I don't understand why Terry needs to see me; he can feel me—isn't that enough? I don't even look at myself in the mirror when I'm getting dressed. I just don't like being naked, and I

59

don't see why you think that's another step in my healing. We're able to have sex, so what's the big deal?"

On the surface, Susan's question made perfect sense. She and Terry were able to complete the act, she had given birth to a daughter and a son, and for the most part memories of her abuse were no longer triggered during sexual relations with her husband. However, the shame she felt about her body and the degree to which she was divorced from her femininity indicated there was more progress to be made if she was willing to pursue it.

One of the consequences of sexual abuse is that survivors often evidence awkwardness with their gender identity. In Susan's case, there was little about the way she carried herself that indicated she was distinctly female versus just an androgynous person. She certainly did not *celebrate* her femininity—her hair was in an unkempt pageboy style, her figure quite out of shape and hidden underneath a wardrobe consisting almost entirely of sweatshirts and sweatpants. She wore no makeup or jewelry, not out of religious convictions but simply because she considered them a nuisance. Her posture and gait were decidedly unflattering, and, in short, there was very little about her that reflected the beauty of God's image to the world.

In subsequent sessions, she and Terry both began to understand how Susan had distanced herself from her femininity as a largely unconscious defense mechanism against her cousin and other boys. It made sense—if she didn't make herself particularly attractive, she didn't have to fend off male advances. Unfortunately, she also forfeited a big part of her uniqueness as God's child—the fun of being female and the spirit of playfulness not just in enjoying clothes, shoes, makeup, jewelry, hairstyles, and manicures, but in bringing beauty to her world through decorating her home, tending a flower garden, dressing up her kids, or adding her feminine touch to whatever she did. It was as if her life were lived in black and white instead of full color.

Terry, likewise, began to recognize that he had not embraced much of his masculine identity. He did little to attend to his body or make himself attractive to Susan. He was a self-described couch potato and took a fairly passive approach to life, being viewed in the business world as a Caspar Milquetoast. This may have been the reason Susan did not feel threatened by him when they began dating. Unfortunately, she now complained that he was apathetic about his roles as provider and protector and that he had no clear vision for his family. In many ways he was the antithesis of a man like King David—"a man after God's own heart"—or of the Lover in the Song of Songs.

It's not surprising that this eschewing of masculinity and femininity was reflected in a sex life that both partners described as pretty bland and unsatisfying. They rarely had sexual relations, and, when they did, it felt obligatory. Terry sometimes just masturbated because it was easier for both of them. Absent was any of the passion and sensuality so evident in the Song of Songs.

It is easy to stereotype masculine and feminine characteristics, and certainly there is great variety in how these can be manifested while still honoring God's design. Also, there is no question that men and women share many of the qualities of both genders, and that is as it should be. However, God did create some differences in males and females, and, in spite of the efforts of some within our culture to neutralize them, these qualities are apparent throughout Scripture in numerous depictions of godly people. It is a beautiful thing to see a vivid representation of godly masculinity or femininity; we do not do justice to our design as bearers of God's image when we are essentially androgynous.

God's Design

In chapter 3 we touched on some of the foundations of a theology of sexuality. Much of that study was drawn directly from Scripture. In this chapter we will consider an additional source for understanding

God's intentions—our own body. God left many clues about his heart for sexual union in the way he designed our physical body.

Procreation

The first and most powerful of these clues to God's intention is found in our procreative ability. God designed sexual union as the means by which we can participate in his greatest work—the creation of new life. Certainly God could have developed another means of reproduction, but he chose to give us a beautiful picture of love, expressed through the giving of ourselves in covenant relationship, resulting in new life. This images the work of his Holy Spirit, who enters us as we receive Christ into ourselves, generating new life within our being.[1]

This book is not principally about sex for procreation but about sex as a means of expressing and strengthening love: lovemaking. Sexual union results in a child only a few times in our life; the vast majority of times it is simply an opportunity to commune with each other in love, to renew and strengthen our bond. But we must never lose sight of God's crowning purpose for it. Malachi 2:15 says, "Has not the LORD made them one? In flesh and spirit they are his. And why one? *Because he was seeking godly offspring.*" God has his children through us. What an awesome, unspeakable privilege!

> **We image God through procreation.**

Complementary Bodies

A second clue to God's heart for sexual union is that our bodies are complementary—they are designed to fit together. Not only so but, unlike most species of animal that must enter from behind, we are able to face each other in the marital embrace, kissing, caressing, and talking face-to-face. We can behold each other, naked and unashamed, and gaze into each other's eyes as we make love.

Many couples fail to take advantage of this ability to see each other. Dr. David Schnarch, a secular sex therapist, tells of designing a book cover and being unable to find a single photo of a couple kissing with their eyes open. He observes that it is as if, at the moment we are about to kiss, we automatically close our eyes, as we do before sneezing. Many people find it extremely difficult to look into their spouse's eyes as they kiss, and even more difficult as they actually begin to make love, becoming nearly impossible at the point of climax. Gazing into our spouse's eyes makes us incredibly vulnerable.

> **As we become one, we can peer into our mate's soul through his or her eyes.**

But what a privilege God has given us in his design! If we are willing, *we can peer into the soul of our mate through his or her eyes as we become one.* We can talk and laugh and cry with him or her as, through the years, we learn to surrender more and more of ourselves in this most intimate exchange of body, soul, and spirit. God intended us to experience a much deeper connection, a *knowing* of each other, than we often do in our lovemaking.

Perhaps this is why, when God refers to sexual union in Scripture, he sometimes uses the word that means "to know" (*yada* in Hebrew or *ginosko* in Greek). This word is filled with covenant meaning. It is a deeply intimate knowing that reflects oneness with each other and not simply head knowledge. Genesis 4:1 (NKJV) reads: "Now Adam *knew* Eve his wife, and she conceived and bore Cain"; and in verse 17: "Cain *knew* his wife, and she conceived and bore Enoch."

In a nonsexual but powerfully intimate way, God says to the prophet Jeremiah, "Before I formed you in the womb I *knew* you"

(Jer. 1:5). This same depth of intimate, relational knowledge is reflected in Matthew 7:22–23 when Jesus states, "Many will say to me on that day, 'Lord, Lord, did we not prophesy in your name, and in your name drive out demons and perform miracles?' Then I will tell them plainly, 'I never *knew* you.'" It is terribly sobering to realize how easily we can say the right words and go through the motions while still failing to establish a truly intimate relationship. May God help us open our eyes to really knowing each other.

Erogenous Zones

A third clue to God's heart for sexuality is found in our erogenous zones. These are bundles of nerves he placed throughout our body that are not necessary for intercourse but that, when gently touched or firmly caressed, can generate a great deal of sexual arousal and pleasure. Most of these areas are never touched by anyone other than our spouse, which makes them another private delicacy to be enjoyed as couples grow in intimacy.

> **God designed our erogenous zones.**

In his best-selling book *A Celebration of Sex,* my friend and colleague Dr. Doug Rosenau breaks these zones down into three levels based on their degree of sensitivity in producing sexual arousal. Level one erogenous zones are obvious: the nipples and genitals. The nerve endings in these areas are extremely sensitive to stimulation, but a skilled lover knows not to focus on them too quickly, allowing passion to build instead by pleasuring levels two and three first.

Level two includes many seemingly unusual areas: the backs of the knees, inner thighs, armpits and chest area, abdomen, the small of the back, neck, the palms of the hands and soles of the feet, the face, temples, and the mouth and tongue. These areas are highly sensitive to stimulation with the fingers, hands, mouth, or tongue and, again, they are areas that no one else is likely to touch—certainly not in an erotic manner. The vulnerability a partner displays in allowing his or her spouse to focus on these zones, and the privilege a partner has in being invited to explore them, is intensely bonding and intimate.

Level three actually includes the entire body with its skin and nerve endings. Our bodies are designed to hunger for touch and to be held, and yet many times we fight against that desire because of discomfort with our bodies or because of past trauma that left us afraid of being vulnerable. Scripture encourages us to risk that kind of vulnerability and to soak up every part of each other's body. The Lover in the Song of Songs expresses his delight in these areas specifically: her head, temples, hair, eyes, nose, teeth, lips and mouth, neck, breasts, waist, navel, legs, and feet. She expresses her enjoyment of him in like manner. This is full-body enjoyment!

When I speak on this passionate enjoyment of every part of our body, I am often asked if I think passionate or so-called French kissing is appropriate for Christians. My response is simply that the Song of Songs *begins* with the invitation, "Let him kiss me with the kisses of his mouth" (1:2). These are not the kisses of the lips—she wants *passionate* kissing! The Lover says, "Your lips drop sweetness as the honeycomb, my bride; milk and honey are under your tongue" (4:11). Later he states, "The fragrance of your breath [is] like apples, and your mouth like the best wine"; to which she responds, "May the wine go straight to my lover, flowing gently over lips and teeth" (7:8–9). These are highly sensual passages and they confirm once again that God knew what he was giving us when he designed our bodies for sexuality, and he delights when we enjoy them with our spouse.

Our Genitalia

A fourth set of clues about God's heart for sex lies in the makeup of our genitalia. Figure 4.1 represents fetal genital development at about six weeks' gestation. It shows a mass of tissue containing nerve endings, but the gender is undifferentiated. At this point, we could not tell male from female without looking at the DNA. Both male and female begin with the same basic equipment: the glans area, urethral fold, lateral buttress, and anal pit—the same tissue, same nerve endings.

We are fearfully and wonderfully made.

Genital Development In Utero
Before the Sixth Week (Undifferentiated)

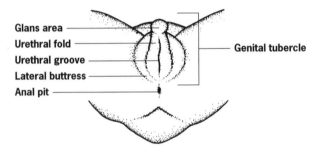

Fig. 4.1

In the seventh to eighth week we begin to see some differentiation (see figure 4.2). In the male we see what will become the head of the penis. In the female that same glans area will differentiate into the head of the clitoris. The vertical midline on the male is starting to close up and will eventually form a kind of raised "seam" along the scrotum and a dark line on the underside of the penis that looks as if a cut had been sutured. That same area will remain open in the female, forming the opening of the vagina. The urethral opening (through which urine will pass) will exit at the head of the penis in the boy, whereas it remains in the middle of the labial opening in the girl, above the vagina and below the clitoris. The lateral buttress will become part of the shaft of the penis in the boy and part of the labia or lips of the vagina in the girl.

Genital Development In Utero
In the Seventh to Eighth Week

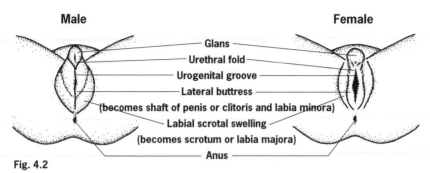

Fig. 4.2

By the twelfth week we can easily tell which is male and which is female (see figure 4.3). The gonads are up inside the boy and will become the testicles, descending into the scrotum around the thirty-second week. The gonads will remain inside the girl's body and become her ovaries.

Genital Development In Utero
At the Twelfth Week (Fully Developed)

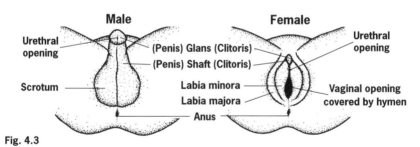

Fig. 4.3

The complexity of our sexual functioning is beyond comprehension (let alone the functioning of our entire body). We can echo the psalmist in saying, "I praise you because I am fearfully and wonderfully made; your works are wonderful, I know that full well" (Ps. 139:14). But in addition to allowing us to marvel at God's design for procreation, this analysis reveals an amazing insight into God's heart for sex. Recall that the material that formed the head of the penis in the male became the head of the clitoris in the female. What is the purpose of the clitoris? It is a small bundle of very sensitive nerve endings that serves absolutely no function in procreation. Its only function is facilitating orgasm in a woman. What does this say about God's interest in our sexual pleasure?

God designed our orgasms.

The female of no other species has orgasms—only humans. Think about that! What a statement about God's heart. Orgasms are an intense experience of pleasure marked by involuntary spasms of the muscles throughout the pubic area, heightened cardiac function and respiration, sharpening of all five senses through a flooding of adrenaline, and a release of endorphins and other highly pleasurable neurochemistry in the brain. We are extremely subject to bonding or pairing during sexual arousal and orgasm (more on this in chapter 8). Within Christian marriage, the ability for both partners to experience orgasms can create a powerful bonding with each other. God designed us to facilitate that!

God placed more nerve endings in the penis and clitoris (not the vagina, the clitoris) than in any other part of the body except the tongue. Again, what does this say about his interest in our pleasure? The same God who equipped us to celebrate his goodness through the enjoyment of rich foods and feasts also equipped us to enjoy a sensual feast with each other in the marital bedroom.

Why do we so rarely teach couples about this when they are preparing for marriage? If we tell them anything at all, it is usually about the penis and vagina. That is part of it—that is how intercourse occurs and how a baby is made. But if we want God's fuller design for sexual union, we must also talk about the role of the clitoris. I have had numerous women complain of never experiencing orgasm and discovered that they didn't even know where the clitoris was. Many who do know about it gained their knowledge from the culture, and with it came a lot of secular distortions. Christians need to do a better job of preparing couples by giving them the full plan of God's heart for bonding spirit, soul, and body. He created sex, and what he created he has pronounced *very good.*[2]

A final thought on this: Most of us have heard about certain Third World countries in which clitorectomies are performed. In this horrendous procedure, the clitoral area is cut out entirely because of a belief that it is wrong for a woman to experience sexual pleasure. It is a sad truth that many Christians have unintentionally performed *psychological* clitorectomies on women (and therefore on couples) by not talking about the importance of the clitoris. Admittedly it is an awkward subject, but its presence in a woman provides an incredible window into God's heart and offers another experience of bonding in lovemaking that can cement the unity of a marriage.

Celebrating Masculinity and Femininity

These four characteristics of sexual functioning—the generation of new life as the manifestation of our love, the design of the marital embrace for deep connecting, our erogenous zones for soaking each other up, and our orgasms for powerful bonding—give us a clear picture of God's heart for sexuality. He designed us to enjoy a feast in body, soul, and spirit, celebrating and renewing our oneness as we glorify and image our Creator.

> **We image God through our masculinity and femininity.**

This understanding provides a great incentive for becoming more passionate lovers. Just as we love impassioned praise and worship music on Sunday morning and passionate preaching from the pulpit, we should enjoy passionate lovemaking in the bedroom. To do so, however, we must become more comfortable with our bodies, and this takes us back to the case of Susan and Terry at the beginning of this chapter. Celebrating and glorifying God with our bodies requires that we embrace and express our masculinity and femininity.

Masculine reflections of God include wisdom, strength, courage, protection, provision, guidance, instruction, and discipline. Feminine reflections are beauty, splendor, praise, attention, patience, nurturance, comfort, and healing. When expressed in love, these qualities balance each other and have a drawing or wooing effect on children and others who know us, just as the Holy Spirit woos us to the Father and the Son. The couple who manifests them is a lighthouse to the world as Jesus called us to be.

Most of these qualities are evidenced in our character, being shaped as we mature in Christ and die to self so that he becomes everything and we nothing. Strength and beauty, however, are also *physical* qualities, which unfortunately are becoming less common in the church and the culture at large. Many of us are terribly out of shape; we are taking less and less care of our bodies. More of our children are obese than at any previous point in history.

I am not suggesting that we pursue the worldly perceptions of masculine strength or feminine beauty so tastelessly displayed on magazine covers. There is a vast difference between taking care of our bodies and having our whole world revolve around them. Men can stay in decent shape without becoming "muscle heads"; women can do likewise without crash dieting and plastic surgery. It simply requires a measure of discipline and moderation—avoiding extremes.

Remember that our bodies are the temple of the Holy Spirit. The temple in the Old Testament was an indescribably beautiful structure—one of the greatest architectural wonders of the ancient world. It was to be carefully maintained as the dwelling place of God. Our bodies are the same; we mustn't let them atrophy from poor diet and lack of activity while offering the excuse that we are just getting older. Certainly our bodies will age; we will have stretch marks, cellulite, surgical scars, and thinning of the skin, but we dishonor God when we are lax in "temple maintenance," and we dishonor our spouse as well. Our bodies are not our own; they are a gift we give to each other.[3] We should want our partner to be pleased with our gift, imperfect as it is.

This temple maintenance also includes our manner of dress. Just three generations ago people dressed for dinner; even college students dressed to go to the dining hall—men wearing dinner jackets and women wearing dresses. I am not suggesting a return to that, but we used to take greater pride in our dress; even gas station attendants and garbage men wore uniforms! Restaurants used to keep spare ties on hand, requiring men to wear them if they came underdressed for dinner. People chose attire and hair-styles that were attractive, and attention was paid to posture, good manners, and social graces. *We used to try harder to look good.*

Even for Sunday morning service or when going out on a date or to a nice restaurant, it is not uncommon now for people to wear T-shirts and shorts. While I am aware that some churches have adopted casual dress as a means of appealing more to the lost, it's fair to say that our dressing down generally has more to do with laziness than with trying to be salt and light. Forgive me for sounding old-fashioned, but it's possible to be casual without looking like we don't care, and comfortable without looking like we just rolled out of bed.

On the flip side of the equation, many women who do pay attention to their clothes and self-care end up dressing provoca-tively. There is a big difference between dressing *attractively* and dressing *seductively.* We can be tastefully beautiful without being openly sexy, just as we can dress modestly without appearing prudish. It simply requires paying attention to classic style and beauty and checking our motives.

Remember, not only are we God's holy temple, but we are created in his image. Our masculinity and femininity are reflections of God to the world.[4] A man strong in body and character who daily lays down his life in love for his wife and children is an irresistible image of the Father. A woman beautiful in body and character who devotedly loves her husband and children is a radiant likeness of him whose very nature is love. The covenant union of these two, which grows stronger through the years, is a glorious picture of the promised consummation of Christ and his bride, the church, for all eternity.

We can see God in our sexuality.

We have now looked at how Scripture and our understanding of the creation of our bodies can be used in developing a very basic theology of sex. Although much more is needed to establish a complete theology, we are at least clearer on God's intentions for his gift. In the next part, we will lay out a detailed model for how to make this vision of God's intentions a reality. If we can experience sexuality as a pure and beautiful thing within marriage, not only can we glorify God through it, but we can come to know him more deeply. By shedding our fears and unbiblical legalisms, we can see more of the beauty, mystery, passion, and power of the Almighty. Sexual theologian Christopher West reminds us of the connection between our heart and how we view our sexuality by quoting Matthew 5:8: "Blessed are the pure in heart, for they will see God." May God give us that purified vision!

Questions for Couples

- How comfortable are you with your body in the marital bedroom? Why?
- How does the thought that God designed your erogenous zones and orgasms change the way you think and feel about them?
- Are there improvements you would like to make in the maintenance of your temple?
- Are there ways in which you would like to improve your imaging of God through your masculinity or femininity and/or through your love for your spouse?

Part 2

A Practical Model

5

The Lovemaking Cycle

The Bible reveals that every part of man's physical life is closely connected with sin or with salvation, and that anything that sin has put wrong, Jesus Christ can put right. We are dealing with soul as it expresses itself through the body. The organs of the body are used as indicators of the state of the spiritual life.

Oswald Chambers

"I just want you to know it's embarrassing as heck to be here right now," Daniel said with a bit of a smile. "If you had told me several years ago that I'd be sitting in a counselor's office telling him about my sex life, I'd have said you were crazy. I figured I knew everything I needed to know about sex. I don't mean I'm like Joe Stud or anything, but in my pre-Christian days I read *Playboy* sometimes, and I was more experienced than I should have been when I got married, if you know what I mean. I thought I was a pretty good lover, but my wife would probably tell you otherwise at this point."

Daniel was a bright and immediately likeable guy. He was thirty-two years old, married for six years, and had a three-year-old son. He had come to see me on his own without any prompting from his wife—rather rare for a man. He quickly explained that his marriage was solid and that he loved his wife, Sandy, very much but was frustrated over feeling that he wasn't a good lover. His primary complaint was premature ejaculation, which often left Sandy feeling neglected in their lovemaking.

As we talked, it became obvious that Dan had a fairly adolescent perspective of sex, which had been shaped largely by magazines and the locker-room wisdom of his non-Christian buddies. For years before his marriage, this adolescent perspective had been paired with periodic masturbation while fantasizing and occasionally using pornography. Sex was fairly physical for him and, though he did truly love Sandy, he was much more tuned into his enjoyment of her in the bedroom than into how he could please her. He wasn't even particularly aware of what things turned her on, although he seemed to think she really liked his bikini briefs.

Over the next few sessions we explored various pieces of God's vision for sexuality as presented in this book. Dan began to see sex as more than just a personal buzz, or as a pass/fail performance for his wife. He began to connect it with the rest of their relationship and to his relationship with God. In so doing, he discovered that he was less focused on himself and his own pleasure in bed. His adolescent view of sex matured into seeing it as a powerful means of expressing his love for Sandy. He began to talk more openly with her and to discover her likes and dislikes. (What a shock to learn that she didn't particularly like his bikini briefs!)

Sandy eventually insisted on joining him in our sessions because she couldn't believe what a change had taken place, not just in their sex life but in the way he was treating her throughout the day. "He's really changing, and I can hardly believe it," she said. "It's like I'm getting a new husband! He's even showing a greater interest in spiritual things. I feel more connected to Danny and like I'm getting to know a side of him I never saw before. I knew it was in there, but it seemed buried or something."

Dan's willingness to seek help for a relatively simple sexual complaint opened a precious window for growth in himself and his marriage. A real maturation process took place. He found that by being more tuned into Sandy in the bedroom and allowing sex to become more relational instead of purely physical, not only did he have greater control over his climaxes, but Sandy began to initiate lovemaking—something she had never done before.

"It's like I finally get what sex is about," Dan said in one of our final sessions. "I can't believe that after almost seven years together we can be enjoying each other more now than we did on our honeymoon."

"It's true," Sandy confirmed. "Our sex life and our whole marriage keeps getting better. One of my girlfriends at church last week commented that she wished her marriage was like ours!"

Daniel and Sandy experienced some of the transformational growth that can occur when a couple begins to really work on their ability to love, honor, and cherish each other on every plane of their marriage, including the sexual. This is not an overstatement. The vulnerability of the marital bedroom makes it the ideal place for developing character and maturity as "iron sharpens iron" and couples learn to give and receive the most intimate expressions of love.

One of the primary tools I use with couples to help them catch a vision for this kind of relational transformation is a model I developed called the Lovemaking Cycle. It incorporates pieces of models developed by sex therapists and researchers over the past several decades but expands to address the relational and spiritual aspects of lovemaking that are the focus of this book.

Stages of Sexual Response

Dr. William Masters and Virginia Johnson are perhaps America's most well-known sex researchers. Although their research methods were less than moral by Christian standards, their findings have provided the foundation for much of the subsequent work in this field. In *Human Sexual Response* (1966) they detailed four stages of sexual response that they identified as *excitement, plateau, orgasm,* and *resolution.* These stages are distinguished from one another by changes occurring in the male and female bodies throughout foreplay and intercourse. These stages can be represented graphically, as shown in the figure below, to give us a model of physiological sexual response.

Masters and Johnson's Four Stages of Sexual Response

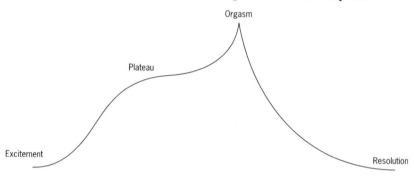

Fig. 5.1

At each stage specific changes occur that help propel the body into the next stage. In *excitement* the heart rate and respiration of both partners increase significantly, often causing their skin to become slightly flushed. The penis, clitoris, and nipples become erect and the vagina begins to lubricate. The genitalia become fully prepared to facilitate intercourse. As penetration occurs and thrusting begins, the couples' bodies reach a *plateau* of sorts in a highly aroused state, preparing for orgasm.

At the point of *orgasm* a group of muscles throughout the entire pubic region goes into involuntary spasm. Ejaculation occurs at this point in the male. Orgasm may occur for the woman during intercourse, but about two-thirds of all women require direct clitoral stimulation to achieve climax. This stimulation can be facilitated before, during, or after intercourse.

Immediately following orgasm the body transitions back to its prearousal state, which is called the *resolution* stage. Blood flow becomes less concentrated in the genitals, muscles relax, and respiration and cardiac function return to normal. The woman can be brought back to orgasm at this point, even multiple times, but the man's body remains in a refractory phase during which a second orgasm is not immediately possible. (The length of this refractory phase generally increases with age, from a few minutes to as much as a few days.)

Not Just Having Sex

The Masters and Johnson model provides a helpful picture of how the body responds to sexual cues; it portrays how human beings function physiologically when having sex. But we are interested in making love, not simply having sex. God has much more in store for his children than just a physical rush. We want to plug this physiological model into a more comprehensive one that incorporates the mental, emotional, relational, and spiritual aspects of making love.

> **God has much more in store for his children than just a physical rush.**

The Lovemaking Cycle is not linear but circular. It places sex within the context of a committed marital relationship and shows it flowing out of the love and intimacy a couple shares on every other plane of their marriage.

Each phase or quadrant of their lovemaking flows into the next and feeds a continuation and deepening of their love.

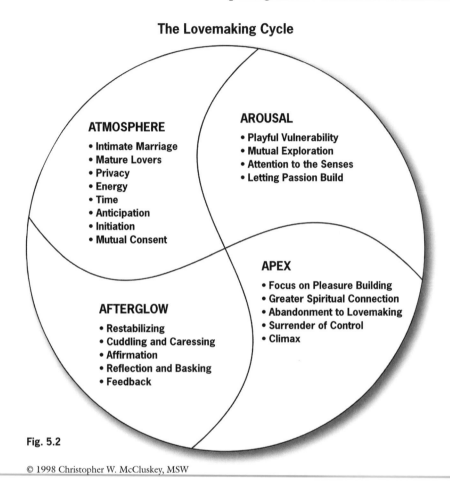

The Lovemaking Cycle

ATMOSPHERE
- Intimate Marriage
- Mature Lovers
- Privacy
- Energy
- Time
- Anticipation
- Initiation
- Mutual Consent

AROUSAL
- Playful Vulnerability
- Mutual Exploration
- Attention to the Senses
- Letting Passion Build

APEX
- Focus on Pleasure Building
- Greater Spiritual Connection
- Abandonment to Lovemaking
- Surrender of Control
- Climax

AFTERGLOW
- Restabilizing
- Cuddling and Caressing
- Affirmation
- Reflection and Basking
- Feedback

Fig. 5.2

© 1998 Christopher W. McCluskey, MSW

If the cycle is thought of as a wheel, and if each piece of the wheel is functioning as it should, a couple's lovemaking will roll along nicely down the road of their lives together. Like exercising a muscle, their marital bond will be strengthened and their sense of oneness deepened each time they move through the cycle. Just as in physics, which states that an object in motion will remain in motion unless acted on by another force, the wheel of a couple's lovemaking will tend to stay in motion throughout their years together unless acted on by some other force.

However, if a piece of their relationship or sexuality is impaired or missing in some way, the wheel of their lovemaking will "clunk" every time it hits that place. If the problem is not addressed, the wheel can eventually clunk to the point that lovemaking stops altogether. This was the case with many of the couples who came to my therapy office. Their relational intimacy had become impaired because of some issue they didn't know how to work through, and the problem had worsened to the point that their love life had come to a standstill. Again, as in physics, an object at rest tends to stay at rest.

Many times all that is required to get the wheel of lovemaking rolling again is to address a few key areas. This model becomes helpful, then, not only in offering a vision of what lovemaking can be but in providing a diagnostic tool for determining where problems may be impairing the lovemaking process. These problems can be targeted for healing and growth so a couple's love life becomes everything God intends it to be.

A quick overview of the model will help to clarify it, and the next four chapters will explore each of the quadrants in far greater detail. True lovemaking always begins within a healthy and God-honoring context or *Atmosphere*. This can occur only within a covenantal marriage as was discussed in chapter 3—not within a dating relationship or for a couple that is living together, which God calls fornication; not within a homosexual relationship, which God calls an abomination; and not within a relationship outside of marriage, which God calls adultery. It can occur only when one man and one woman are in a covenant marriage for life.

That is not the only requirement for a healthy Atmosphere, however. There are many Christian couples whose marriages and lives are anything but conducive to an intimate and fulfilling sex life. A couple must be mature and able to share intimately on all

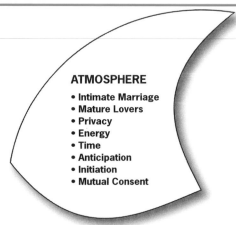

ATMOSPHERE

• Intimate Marriage
• Mature Lovers
• Privacy
• Energy
• Time
• Anticipation
• Initiation
• Mutual Consent

Fig. 5.3

other planes of their relationship. As the title of the classic book by Dr. Kevin Leman suggests, *Sex Begins in the Kitchen—Because Love Is an All-Day Affair.* Sexual love should always be a *confirmation* of the love that has been expressed throughout the day.

A couple must also have healthy boundaries around their privacy, energy, and time. They must allow themselves to mentally anticipate and prepare for their times of sexual intimacy. They need to be able to talk about their desires and at times negotiate with each other when their interests vary. There must be mutual respect that never allows sex to become an issue of control or a weapon used to punish the other.

When the key ingredients of a healthy, godly Atmosphere are in place and when a couple has mutually consented to a specific time of lovemaking, they will roll into the second quadrant of the model, *Arousal.* Here they will tune into their own and their partner's body in a spirit of playfulness, as clothing is removed and they explore each other. Allowing various stimuli to flood their senses, they will talk and tease and connect with each other's body, soul, and spirit, becoming physically, emotionally, and spiritually naked and vulnerable. While embracing the gift of their sexuality and inviting their passion to build, they spill naturally down into the third quadrant.

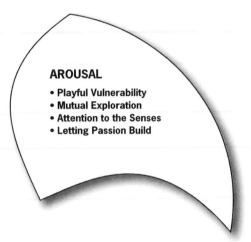

Fig. 5.4

The third quadrant, called the *Apex*, is marked by the couple abandoning themselves to lovemaking, allowing their passion to carry them to a point of tremendous connectedness. They lose all inhibitions as their bodies are joined and they surrender themselves completely to climax. Time seems to stand still for a few precious moments. They are alone as one.

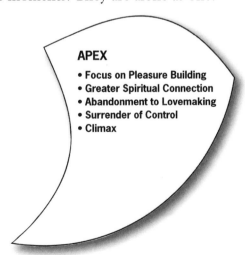

Fig. 5.5

The Apex is followed immediately by a phase I call *Afterglow*. This is a period when the partners collect themselves after their experience of surrender. It corresponds physiologically to Masters and Johnson's *resolution* stage, when the couple's bodies are returning to normal. During this phase, there is a wonderful opportunity for the lovers to bask in what they have just shared by cuddling, caressing, and verbally affirming the love they have communicated with their bodies. It is a time of soaking up the joy of their oneness and reflecting on the relationship, becoming aware at an even deeper level of how intimate the marriage has become. The two praise each other and compare notes on what they enjoyed and perhaps what they wish to change next time. This basking and sharing encourages them to make provision for lovemaking again as they return to the Atmosphere quadrant.

AFTERGLOW

• **Restabilizing**
• **Cuddling and Caressing**
• **Affirmation**
• **Reflection and Basking**
• **Feedback**

Fig. 5.6

Our purpose here is to provide only a brief overview of the Lovemaking Cycle—a picture of what couples can experience in their sexuality. We will now begin to look at each quadrant in detail and identify keys to enhancing the function of each, as well as point out problem areas and suggest ways to alleviate them. Lovemaking is filled with opportunities for ever-deepening experiences of oneness but is also fraught with potential for breakdowns and disconnection. We encourage you to read through the following chapters in order and to discuss them as a couple in pursuit of more of the fullness of God's plan for your sexual union.

Questions for Couples

- ❧ Are there ways in which immaturity and self-centeredness are keeping your lovemaking stuck at a fairly physical level?
- ❧ At what point(s) does sexual intercourse feel most connected to the rest of your relationship? When does it feel most disconnected?
- ❧ Are you committed to beginning a more open dialogue about your sex life as a couple?
- ❧ What aspect(s) of lovemaking would you most like to improve as you continue reading?

6

Atmosphere

Creating an Environment Conducive to Lovemaking

Nothing, not even the best and noblest, can go on as it is now.
Nothing, not even what is lowest and most bestial, will not be
raised again if it submits to death. It is sown a natural body, it
is raised a spiritual body. Flesh and blood cannot come to the
Mountains. Not because they are too rank, but because they are
too weak. . . . Lust is a poor, weak, whimpering, whispering thing
compared with that richness and energy of *desire* which will arise
when lust has been killed.

C. S. Lewis

You could have cut the tension with a knife. I hated sessions like
this. Tom sat in his chair, arms folded and jaw set, an angry scowl
on his face. I'm not sure he even bowed his head as I opened in
prayer. Judy sat on the couch with a sofa pillow clasped in her arms,
as if she were trying to hide. She seemed afraid to even look up.

"I don't see that we really have much to discuss here," Tom began. "Scripture addresses this as clear as day, just as it does any other problem."

Tom was chairman of the board of deacons at his church and had already made sure that I knew he filled in for his pastor sometimes when he was out of town. It became quickly obvious that he had memorized vast amounts of Scripture. No matter what issue we raised, he had a chapter and verse to quote, which he felt addressed it. I couldn't help thinking of Jesus listening to the Pharisees.

"We're here because Judy has become hardened of heart and stiff-necked. She is not submissive to my headship and has begun to refuse me in the marital debt. First Corinthians 7, verse 5, says, 'Do not deprive each other except by mutual consent and for a time, so that you may devote yourselves to prayer. Then come together again so that Satan will not tempt you because of your lack of self-control.'

"Judy is withholding herself from me. You are supposedly a Christian brother, so I am bringing this to you as Scripture tells us to when someone is in sin."

It is hard to know even where to begin with couples like this, and I have seen many. I have gotten to the point that, when I hear 1 Corinthians 7:4–5 being quoted, I know where the conversation is going and my spirit becomes immediately burdened. True, these verses are in God's Word and are therefore truth, but the spirit in which they are often used is so far from God's heart. Love does not demand (see 1 Cor. 13:5). How it must grieve the Spirit when we pervert God's Word for our own selfish purposes!

For a couple to enter into the joy of God's gift of marital sexuality, they must first establish an environment or atmosphere that is conducive to freely giving and receiving love. For this reason, the Lovemaking Cycle begins with Atmosphere and identifies several key factors that must be present to create this kind of environment. We will address each in some detail in this chapter.

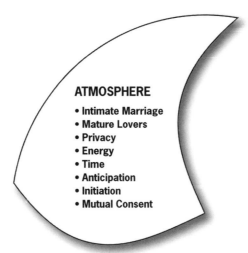

ATMOSPHERE

- Intimate Marriage
- Mature Lovers
- Privacy
- Energy
- Time
- Anticipation
- Initiation
- Mutual Consent

Fig. 6.1

Intimate Marriage

We have already noted that lovemaking as God designed it is rooted in a healthy covenantal marriage. This does not mean a perfect marriage but one in which both partners are completely committed to each other for life and to being known, which means being real, transparent, and intimate with each other. Their relationship is built on trust, requiring absolute honesty. They are not afraid of each other—of being harmed, belittled, cheated on, or deserted. They know that the marriage is grounded in the Lord and that they can lean into it when they need strength and it will sustain them.

Sexual union is the outgrowth and expression of these things. If these characteristics are not present, the couple is not ready for the rest of this model. They need to focus on healing and growth in their ability to love each other in nonsexual ways first. A marriage cannot facilitate lovemaking if it is marred by uncertain commitment, lack of transparency, a controlling spirit, or dishonesty (all of which breed *fear*). *The couple may have sex but they will not be able to make love, because the spirit is wrong.* "There is no fear in love" (1 John 4:18).

Mature Lovers

Let's look at the components of an intimate marriage: the two individuals. They relate well as a couple, but there are other aspects we must consider. Are they *mature* as individuals? Are they not only intimate but also growing? As Christians, are they dying to self and growing into Christ's likeness? Are they developing a gentle, compassionate spirit, full of grace and mercy? Do they communicate honestly their thoughts, feelings, and desires? Are they servants? Are they disciplined? Are they learning how to give and how to receive? These are some of the signs of a mature individual.

> **Making love requires maturity and a loving heart.**

Making love requires maturity and a loving heart. Mature individuals can delay gratification because their desires are in submission to God's Spirit. Maturity recognizes that sometimes the best way to make love is to forego sexual relations and just hold each other or serve the other or talk, cry, or pray together. When a couple views lovemaking as much more than simply completing the sex act, they ensure that when they *are* sexual, their union will be a true reflection of their oneness in the rest of the relationship—it will in fact be the ultimate expression of that truth.

Conversely, mature individuals can consent to sexual relations even when they don't especially feel like it. They do not insist that they always be as interested as their partner, and they never withhold relations as a means of retaliation when there is a disagreement. Maturity knows that sometimes the best way to ease tensions and start mending a relationship is to reidentify a sense of oneness and commitment to working things out by sexually renewing their vows.

These first two elements of Atmosphere in lovemaking—an intimate marriage and mature lovers—provide the foundation for everything else. When they are present, any number of sexual problems that may arise can be worked through. Two mature people who love the Lord and each other can handle anything in him.

But when there is a lack of relational intimacy and/or maturity on the part of one or both spouses, all other problems will be much more difficult to resolve. Relational intimacy and Christian maturity are the raw materials through which marital problems are addressed. When they are absent, problems persist and worsen.

Privacy

The next three aspects of Atmosphere— privacy, energy, and time—are very practical. Looking first at privacy, a couple needs to ask themselves, "Are we able to have time alone together?" As parents of five children, Rachel and I know that privacy can be a rare commodity. We have a fairly intimate marriage between two fairly mature people, but it's difficult to get just the two of us in bed without a couple of kids with teddy bears and bottles joining us. Privacy can be very hard to come by! Many times sexual relations will stall simply because a couple can't find any privacy.

> **If a couple does not make privacy a priority at regular intervals, their sex life will suffer badly.**

Certain boundaries must be in place to ensure time alone to nurture the relationship. This may mean planning date nights when the kids will be with a babysitter or staying overnight with friends or relatives. If an aging parent lives with you, it may mean arranging for respite care. Children must be taught to respect a locked door, and weekly rituals may need to be established to allow for uninterrupted time on Sunday afternoons or days off. If a couple does not make privacy a priority at regular intervals, their sex life will suffer badly.

Energy

The next question couples must ask is similar: "Do we have enough energy by the time we come together sexually?" How many times have you come into the bedroom at the end of a day, closed the door, and said to your spouse, "I can't do another thing. You look great, but I'm dead!" When couples make private time together, they must also have enough energy to enjoy each other, or very little will occur, and what does happen will not satisfy. In our fast-paced lives, energy is often in short supply. Many times sexual relations will be far less than they could be simply because we are so exhausted.

Addressing this problem is a tremendous struggle in Western culture. Countless books have been written on the subject of overload and the importance of simplifying, living by our priorities, managing our time, and learning to say no. Much of the life coaching I do is centered on these two issues of balance and simplicity.

As our former pastor, Dr. Bill Anderson, often said, "The enemy of the best is most often the good." If couples desire fulfilling sexual relations for the benefit of their marriage, they must practice saying no occasionally to many other good things. They may have to go to bed earlier, step down from extracurricular activities, draw healthier boundaries to reduce stress, or even cut back on work hours. But, if they use the energy regained to strengthen their marriage through time together and passionate lovemaking, the sacrifices will produce a wonderful payoff.

Time

Another very practical aspect of Atmosphere is time. Couples must ask, "Can we find any time together when we have both privacy and energy?" Privacy, energy, and time are required if you are to luxuriate in sexual relations instead of just rushing through a "quickie."

In an intimate marriage between mature lovers, there is nothing wrong with the occasional quickie. Sometimes that's the best you can do, and something is usually better than nothing. But, comparing our sexual appetites with our physical appetites, this is like saying that Taco Bell is okay once in a while. You don't want to make a steady diet of Taco Bell—and you don't want to make a steady diet of quickies in your marital relationship. They are not going to satisfy; they will not feed and strengthen you. However, if privacy, energy, and/or time are in short supply, quickies are often what you wind up with—if you have sexual relations at all.

My friend Doug Rosenau, whom I mentioned in chapter 4, tells a story I always think of when I speak on this. He was working with a couple, encouraging them to spend time luxuriating in their lovemaking. They had a vacation coming up, and he said, "That's great, because vacations are such wonderful aphrodisiacs! They're a great time to get away and stop the business and be able to just focus on each other." The couple looked at him, and the wife gently replied, "Dr. Rosenau, obviously you have never vacationed with three small children. Last vacation we did it once, in the bathroom, standing up, and there was a two-year-old knocking on the door!" Can you relate? For truly fulfilling lovemaking we need privacy, we need energy, and we need time.

Anticipation

Next, we need to anticipate. An atmosphere conducive to lovemaking requires that you plan ahead and make provision for time with your spouse. Sex should never become just an afterthought. You need to prepare your body, perhaps through showering or freshening up, and prepare your mind and spirit to be able to give yourself so your body will cooperate. To connect intimately you must be ready to receive as well as to give. You may need to reflect on past times to remind yourself of how wonderful sex feels and how important it is to the overall health of your marriage. One expression of your anticipation will be ensuring that you have the necessary privacy, energy, and time. All of this takes mental awareness and planning.

Dr. Michael Sytsma, another friend and colleague, tells the story of a couple he was counseling. The husband reported having looked at his wife's day planner and noticing she had several days marked with the letters "TS" in red ink. When he inquired as to what "TS" meant, she explained, "Oh, that means 'Think sex!'" She had found that, unless she wrote it in her calendar, often she didn't think about sex more than every couple of weeks. So she decided to train herself to remember more consciously how much she enjoyed that time and how good it was for the two of them, to prepare herself more for it. As funny as it may sound, she insisted that doing so made her more receptive to her husband's advances and even occasionally resulted in her being the initiator.

Anticipation will be more difficult for some people than others, particularly if there is sexual trauma in their background.

Work on reframing any negative thoughts about sex.

These persons may unconsciously try to block thoughts of sex until their partner tries to initiate. At that point it should be no surprise that they may not be very interested or that their body may not respond the way they would desire. They have succeeded in blocking out the very thoughts that would have helped them be responsive. This affects many more couples than we might imagine. Studies indicate that roughly one in four women have experienced sexual abuse by the time they are eighteen, and the numbers are not much better for men.

Even without sexual abuse, many persons will unconsciously block sexual thoughts simply because of negative associations. If they have a poor body image, feeling they are unattractive, they may be averse to thoughts of being naked with their partner. If they were raised to view sex as somehow dirty or bad or wrong, they may struggle greatly with allowing themselves to focus on it. As Christians we are supposed to think on things that are honorable, pure, lovely, and worthy of praise (see Phil. 4:8). If sex is not seen in this light, it may be very difficult to embrace thoughts of it and to fantasize about the next experience of lovemaking. Hopefully this book is providing a fresh understanding of God's heart for sexuality and can help you reframe any negative thoughts. Use the questions at the end of each chapter to further that process.

Initiation

Obviously, making love is a two-person activity. Somehow you have to let your partner know that you are interested and find out if he or she is interested. One of the funniest things I've discovered in counseling is learning how couples initiate with each other. Often their cues are only nonverbal. She always wears a particular negligee, and he knows what that negligee means. Or he always puts on a certain aftershave. Maybe she hates the aftershave, but she knows what he's ready for. Or they fumble around with euphemisms: "Would you like to, you know . . ."

> **There is too much potential for miscommunication and hurt feelings to leave initiation entirely nonverbal.**

Being vulnerable enough to communicate our interest in sexual relations can result in a great deal of awkwardness, especially if our spouse isn't even remotely interested or isn't picking up on our cues. Couples need to wrestle with their sexual language, as we discussed in chapter 2, and come to agreement as to how they will let each other know.

A woman I counseled complained that her husband hadn't responded to her initiation the night before: "I'm standing there with my top off and he just walks right by me! What does he think I want—of course I want to make love!"

I quickly reminded her that in our previous session she had complained, "I can't stand that every time I so much as take my clothes off, he starts wanting to make love!" If we want to communicate something with our bodies that we cannot first communicate with our mouths, we need to back up. We need to be able to talk. There is too much potential for miscommunication and hurt feelings to leave initiation entirely nonverbal.

One of the best ways you can get more comfortable talking about sex is to read a book like this one aloud to each other in bed, not a chapter a night but just a page or two, and if it takes a year to get through it, that's okay. You will get information that may foster your dialogue, and you will also be greatly desensitizing yourselves to those sexual words that are so powerful and awkward. Once you have read the same word aloud twenty-five times with your spouse lying next to you, it's easier to turn to him or her and use that word in a productive discussion. Try this to help desensitize you in healthy ways so you can initiate in a more natural and playful manner.

One of the most fun couples I ever worked with were in their sixties. When I asked how they initiated lovemaking, they gave each other a knowing grin and the wife giggled. She gave him a nod of approval and he answered, "One of my ways is to tell her that Pepe wants to know if Fifi can come out and play!" We all burst out laughing. What a wonderfully fun atmosphere that creates for them coming together to play and rejoice in their oneness! Couples need to agree on creative ways to communicate their interest in being sexual.

Mutual Consent

A final key to an atmosphere conducive to making love is mutual consent. Both parties should come to the marital bed willingly, desiring to be together. Even if they have unresolved issues to work through, they must still in their hearts desire to give themselves completely in celebration and renewal of their oneness. This was one of the key things missing for the couple at the beginning of this chapter. Judy could choose to submit to sex with Tom, but her heart was not in it—she felt controlled and used. There was serious work to do on the other planes of their marriage before they would ever be able to do more than just have sex. Unfortunately, Tom proved unable or unwilling to do that work.

Making love is not "sex for the man." It is not "servicing his need" or "fulfilling the marital debt." I have heard many Christian men and even pastors misuse Scripture to insist on relations, such as Ephesians 5:24 about wives submitting to their husbands or

1 Corinthians 7:4–5, as Tom did. They wield these verses like a club, insisting that their wives must be sexual with them whenever they desire it. I have heard one preacher emphasize, "You never ever, ever, ever, ever, EVER say no!"

A couple being sexual in that kind of spirit are incapable of making love as we have presented it. That is a spirit of taking, not of giving and receiving, and it will eventually become dissatisfying for both the husband and the wife. It is not reflective of Christ and his church, because Christ does not force himself on us. For those couples, sex has become the husband's right and the wife's duty. It is little more than a legalistic act, and in some instances it is a sin—a completely selfish act. She can become for him little more than living pornography, because sex is being used simply to relieve himself. A blunt way of saying it is that she becomes a hole for him to masturbate into. The spirit of the act is entirely wrong. *Remember, when the spirit behind sex is one of lust, selfishness, disobedience, or lies rather than love, Satan is glorified.*

Lovemaking as God intended it is to be a communing of our spirits, not just a servicing of a felt need. If the husband has such a need for sex that he can force his wife to meet that need, what do we say to the poor single who has no one? Is he going to explode? Should he find a sexual outlet outside of marriage? No. We are first and foremost to discipline our bodies; we do not service their every fleshly desire and justify our selfishness by misusing God's Holy Word. Our bodies are to be subject to the guidance of the Holy Spirit. If a spouse is not free to say no to sex, his or her yes becomes meaningless. When a husband or wife is forced into compliance, it is not an expression of love.

If relations are not occurring as frequently as one spouse would like them, the couple needs to begin a dialogue about this *outside of the bedroom.* This is a time when the maturity of both partners is critical. As is often the case, the marriage may be fine, but they simply have differing levels of desire. When this is true, the couple can agree to have relations at times even if one of them isn't especially in the mood and to forgo relations at other times, with neither partner feeling used or spurned. Both decisions are then a true reflection of love.

Lack of desire may indicate that there is a growing emotional distance in the marriage that needs to be addressed. There may be medical issues or stress or depression. Previously unrecognized sexual trauma may be surfacing, which can provide a beautiful opportunity for the other spouse to be used by God as an agent for healing, rather than a tool of the enemy for worsening the damage.

Couples will discover these things only if they engage in what may prove to be some difficult discussions, but the fruit of those discussions can be a much deeper experience of intimacy than could have been had by forcing compliance or fulfilling a duty. Being able to give ourselves freely and completely to each other is the atmosphere for godly lovemaking.

Questions for Couples

- ❧ Would you describe your marriage as fairly intimate? Why or why not? What specific areas could use improvement?

- ❧ Are lack of privacy, energy, and/or time impairing your sexual intimacy? How can you address these issues?

- ❧ In what ways do you and your spouse normally initiate lovemaking? Are there creative ways in which you could expand your repertoire of sexual cues?

- ❧ Are you able to focus on your partner and give him or her the pleasure God designed the body to experience? Are you able to receive that pleasure yourself?

7

Arousal

Embracing Passion

My lover thrust his hand through the latch-opening;
  my heart began to pound for him.
I arose to open for my lover,
  and my hands dripped with myrrh,
my fingers with flowing myrrh,
  on the handles of the lock.

Song of Songs 5:4–5

Rob and Sherry were a fun couple, both in their early thirties, clear-eyed and still full of determination for the dreams they had for the future. Married four years, they had no children but were hoping to start their family in the next year or so after buying a house. Rob worked as a CPA, and Sherry was a teacher finishing her master's degree. They were active in their church, took fairly good care of themselves, and had a healthy social life. It was clear that they loved each other as they sat holding hands on the couch, but there was obvious tension in the air.

Sherry began. "I hope you can help us get past a real sore spot in our marriage. It's getting worse over time instead of better, and we've got to do something about it. It has to do with our sex life, and I understand that's something you specialize in."

I praised their maturity in agreeing to address it together, and Sherry continued. "I don't know how to say this except that ever since the first few months of our marriage, I've felt critiqued by Rob during sex. He doesn't actually say anything, but I can sense his criticism or displeasure, which makes me feel self-conscious and angry. The times I've asked him what's wrong, he says he just wishes I were more active in bed or something. I feel like he's comparing me with his old girlfriend—Rob lived with a woman for a while when he was in college before he became a Christian. We've worked through that and I've forgiven him for the stuff he did before he was saved, but, when we're having sex, I still feel like I'm never living up to whatever she was like. It's like there are three of us in the room instead of just us two."

They'd been facing me to this point, but Rob now turned and looked directly at Sherry, a grieved look on his face. "Honey, I am not comparing you with Tori! I know I did that a couple of times when we were first married, and you know I could kick myself for it—it was one of the stupidest things I've ever done—but I've apologized at least a hundred times. I've told you that was a sick relationship from the get-go and I am infinitely more blessed to be with you than with her! I love you with all my heart, and I wish I'd never been with Tori or any other woman—maybe none of this would have ever been a problem."

Turning to me, he continued. "It's like even though I've apologized and tried to reassure her, we just can't get past that old comparison. It's like Sherry doesn't even like sex anymore, and we're both so tense and guarded in the bed. I feel like anything I do or say makes her feel compared. She's become so passive, and she hardly ever has a climax. I don't want her to be having sex just for my sake—I want us to really enjoy being together!"

I love working with couples like this. It's not that they don't have a problem—they certainly do. Premarital sex always (and I repeat, *always*) creates some degree of problems, with comparison and distorted expectations being some of the most common. But Rob and Sherry were two mature people who truly loved each other. What's more, they loved the Lord and were committed to their marriage and to working this problem through. That's a lot of reason for hope for real change and growth.

This was an intimate marriage between two mature people. Looking at the Lovemaking Cycle, we confirmed that they were able to ensure privacy, energy, and time. They allowed themselves to mentally anticipate, had some fairly clear ways of initiating, and mutually consented to lovemaking. They were fine in the first quadrant of the model. The problems arose as they transitioned into the second quadrant, Arousal.

In this phase, couples begin to allow their bodies to communicate the same message their hearts and lives have expressed throughout the day. This requires tuning out the world and tuning into each other as clothing is removed and they become naked physically, mentally, emotionally, and spiritually. As they begin to caress each other's erogenous zones, their awareness becomes flooded with a plethora of sensory cues.

Playful Vulnerability

As much as our bodies hunger for this kind of touch and our hearts yearn to be ravished, many couples struggle greatly with allowing for it. If there is going to be a breakdown in lovemaking, quadrant two is often where it occurs. This is because the first key ingredient for arousal is a playful vulnerability. We must come to the marital bedroom in the same childlike spirit that Jesus instructed us to come to the Father. This is not a *childishness* but a *child-likeness,* full of curiosity, excitement, and willingness to risk.

To be vulnerable means to become so transparent that we hold nothing back; we become entirely naked physically, emotionally, and spiritually. We give all that we are to our spouse and receive all of who our spouse is, with nothing between us. The antithesis of this is cultures in which sex is viewed so disparagingly that couples *never* see each other naked. I've heard of a group in which couples had sexual relations with a sheet between them with a hole in it to allow for penetration. Although this sounds absurd to us, we can easily create the same effect emotionally and spiritually by giving our body but holding back our soul and our spirit. We can complete the act and never really give our self.

This is a common experience for many couples, because making ourselves vulnerable puts us at risk of being hurt—being spurned or criticized or made to feel foolish. No one wants to experience these things, but, when we try to guard against them, we fail

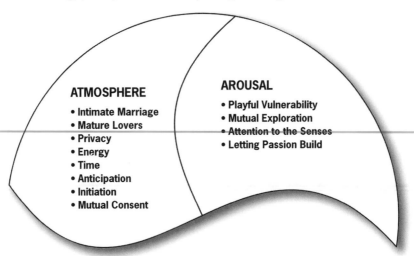

Fig. 7.1

to give ourselves completely in love. We can guard ourselves in many ways, such as only partially disrobing, insisting that all lights be turned off, stifling any talk or sounds of pleasure, focusing on fetishes or fantasies and objectifying our spouse so we don't really connect with him or her, rushing through the act to get it over with, or passively giving our body while our mind turns to other things. Each of these is an example of giving our body while holding back our spirit and soul.

Psychiatrist and author Dr. Eric Berne developed a school of thought in the 1960s called transactional analysis in which he suggested that human beings interact with each other out of three distinct ego states: the parent, the adult, and the child. The parent ego state is the moralistic part of us that discriminates between right and wrong. It serves to keep us in line, to discipline our desires, and to ensure responsible action. Couples interact parent to parent when trying to make important decisions concerning the life of their family. Our parent state helps preserve social order and is largely responsible for growth and maturity throughout life. However, it can also cause unnecessary anxiety if it becomes overly harsh and critical.

The adult ego state is our normal rational mode of operation in adulthood. This is the part of us that, without much debate or hesitation, works a job, pays the bills, cleans the house, raises the children, interacts with neighbors, and basically carries on with life. In a healthy marriage, couples most often interact with each other adult to adult.

The child ego state is the part of us that knows how to have fun. It is the part that allows us to really enjoy life, to be adventurous, to drop our inhibitions and forget ourselves. It is in the child state that we can tease, laugh, play, explore, and be creative. Unfortunately, this is often an uncomfortable and unfamiliar state for many adults who have not allowed themselves to really play since they were children. Couples who want to experience the fullness of God's plan for sexuality must let go of their inhibitions and come to the marital bed child to child.

Instead, many couples come to sex in their critical parent mode, reserved and uptight, wondering if sex is wrong or bad or dirty or a sin. They obsess over their bodies: *How could my partner possibly be turned on by me?* They critique themselves or their spouses and their sexual performance. They may be harsh and demanding, as was the legalistic husband in the previous chapter.

Other couples come to sex in their utilitarian adult mode, still thinking about their jobs, worrying over bills, distracted by the chores they haven't finished. Their sex is fairly staid and almost businesslike. Though they may complete the act, it will be relatively devoid of joy and neither particularly memorable nor bonding. It can feel like simply another thing to do before the day is over.

> **Couples who want to experience the fullness of God's plan for sexuality must let go of their inhibitions and come to the marital bed child to child.**

In the parent or adult modes, joy and spontaneity are dampened and can even be destroyed. Couples become spectators instead of active participants, sitting up on the bedpost instead of frolicking with each other in the bed. This is what had happened to Rob and Sherry. They were both so guarded that they couldn't play. Apologies had been made and forgiveness granted, but they had been unable to come back together in a spirit of play and reckless abandon. As soon as they recognized this, they became more intentional about being playful and found that their lovemaking improved dramatically and rapidly.

It is only in the child state that the passion and wonder of becoming one are set free to join us body, soul, and spirit, unreserved and unashamed. Couples must learn to play with each other. This may require some therapy or counseling if you have areas that need healing, but it may be as simple as scheduling more fun dates and playtime into your lives. Go bike riding or picnicking together, play tennis, see a comedy, double date with another fun couple. Do whatever you enjoy but learn to let go, to risk, to laugh, to squeal, to groan in uninhibited enjoyment of each other.

Mutual Exploration

In that spirit of playful vulnerability, couples begin to explore each other. They may take turns being the initiator and the receiver, or they may explore each other simultaneously, but they must both tune into the other. In the Song of Songs, we have beautiful pictures of "browsing among the lilies" and enjoying all "the choice fruits of her garden,"[1] a couple being together in that intimate place with no barriers between them. Sometimes the Lover is the initiator, and sometimes it is the Beloved.

Remember that this is not "sex for the man." It is very easy for men to consistently play the active role and women the passive, because the sex drive is almost always stronger in the male. Testosterone, the hormone principally responsible for the sex drive, is present in men at roughly fifteen times the level in women. *But once lovemaking is initiated, arousal has more to do with actively inviting passion than it does with hormones.* Couples are encouraged to explore each other with curiosity, fascination, titillation, and teasing.

Many husbands express frustration that their wives are not responsive enough in bed. Certainly this is sometimes due to the wife not tuning into her body and letting herself go, but many times it is because the husband is expecting her to respond in exactly the same way he does. A man's arousal can be fairly simple and physiological, with or without much romance or other emotional connecting. A little physical touching and he can be ready to go. *But God's design for female sexual response requires that a man explore his wife's thoughts and emotions in addition to her body.* Taking a slower, more sensitive and relational approach coaxes a woman out to play rather than requiring her to become instantly aroused by touch alone. It also enables the husband to make love to her whole person and not just to her body, because she is more fully engaged (as is he, by that point). An old French saying suggests, "There are no frigid women, only clumsy men." There is probably some real truth in that! Learn to mutually explore each other—body, soul, and spirit.

Attention to the Senses

As couples tune into and stimulate each other, their attention must shift from the things that could distract them to a growing awareness of their sensate pleasure. Arousal is cued on all five of our senses. This is the most critical aspect of Arousal, and without it couples will not be able to flow into the next quadrant.

Attending to your senses means tuning into sensuality. Sensuality is not a specifically sexual term; it simply means that something is stimulating to the senses. We can understand sensuality by thinking of a nice trip to the beach. We experience the incredible smell of the salt air and the warmth of the sun on our bodies and the hot sand under our feet. We see the beauty of the rolling waves and the horizon, the breathtaking sunsets, the palm trees, and the sea oats blowing in the wind. We feel the surf as it breaks against our legs and enjoy the sensation of being buoyed up on the waves. There is the taste of salt water in our mouths and the sound of gulls in the air, the crashing of the waves, and children laughing. All of our senses are

> **Taking a slower, more sensitive and relational approach coaxes a woman out to play.**

bathed as we soak in these pleasures, and we can stay for hours, enjoying the experience.

Or think of another sensual experience: Thanksgiving dinner. We look forward to it every year. Ah, there's anticipation! Much of the reason we enjoy it is because it is such a feast for our senses. Thanksgiving is much more than a simple meal. It is marked by the sounds of laughter and chatter as family and friends come together, hugging each other and expressing their love. The house is filled with incredible aromas, and we sneak tastes of each dish as it is brought from the kitchen. A visually beautiful banquet is set before us, brimming with tastes and textures. All five of our senses are stimulated as we sate our appetites and enjoy each other's company. What a great time of celebration, and what a wonderful way to worship the Father as we bask in his goodness! God is glorified in our bodies through our sensual feasting.

We would not dream of blocking our enjoyment of these pleasurable sensate stimuli. It would be odd if we didn't want to simply be flooded with them. But blocking is what often happens to couples in sexual union, for a host of reasons. Sensate blocking is more than just not getting turned on. It is consciously or unconsciously working *against* becoming aroused. This can result from a poor body image, negative messages about sex, poor communication, or conflict in the marriage. It can be a reaction to feeling that your spouse is only using you for sex and doesn't really love you. And, clearly, it can be a response to feeling compared to someone else, as in Rob and Sherry's case. No one wants to flood one's awareness with sensual cues that are paired with such messages.

One of the most common reasons for blocking is sexual trauma from the past, because the sensate cues that would normally produce arousal have instead been paired with fear and violation. The unconscious mind will powerfully resist stimuli that can trigger past trauma. This is part of why therapy is so important for survivors of sexual abuse. If we cannot embrace sensuality in the bedroom and allow it to wash over us, our bodies will not respond as we want them to, and we will be robbed of the fullness of what God intended.

I often do an exercise with couples that is helpful in working on arousal. Make a list of all five senses on a piece of paper—sight, smell, taste, touch, and hearing. Next to each, write down all the things you can think of that cue you for sexual arousal. Examples might include the smell of your spouse's perfume or cologne, the taste of her kiss, the sound of his voice, the sight of her legs, the feel of a warm shower, the touch of his fingertips. You might also include less distinctly sexual things such as the glow of moonlight on the water, a gentle evening breeze, soft candlelight, the feel of fresh bed sheets, romantic music, the taste of strawberries dipped in chocolate. A variety of things can cue you for sexual arousal.

Next, make a list of all the things you can think of that turn you off. These might include body odor or bad breath, a crass joke or slang, the feel of razor stubble, a beer gut, an icy cold room. Again, you might include seemingly unrelated things, such as the bloated feeling of having eaten too much, a critical comment made earlier in the day, bright lights, the background noise of the TV, an old worn-out nightgown. You may need to include things that would normally be arousing but which, for you, are paired with past sexual abuse, such as a certain phrase or smell or being touched on a certain part of your body.

What I have found is that sometimes people's list of turnoffs is longer than their list of turn-ons. This is obviously a problem. Perhaps they have never really allowed themselves to think about what gets them aroused, or perhaps they have so many negative impressions about sex that most everything associated with it shuts them down.

As you compare your list with your spouse's, work to increase your incorporation of positive cues and to actively reduce the negative ones. You may find that you can learn to re-pair many of the turnoffs, and they can become turn-ons, as you now cue them to each other and the love that you share. Be sure to claim back anything the enemy has stolen from you through sexual abuse.

As the two of you discuss these admittedly awkward things, expanding your repertoire of turn-ons and eliminating as many turnoffs as you can, recognize that you are greatly enhancing your intimacy as you come to know each other more fully. By choosing to be so transparent and by lovingly responding to each other's desires, you are doing more than just making your sex life better. You are deepening your ability to make love. Very few couples enjoy this level of honesty and vulnerability.

Letting Passion Build

The final ingredient for Arousal is simply to let the passion build. If you recall the Masters and Johnson model discussed in chapter 4, a plateauing stage is reached just prior to orgasm. There comes a point at which you must become somewhat self-focused on the pleasure you are experiencing, inviting and embracing it. This may seem antithetical to the process of connecting with each other, but remember that lovemaking is about giving and receiving. If we remain so focused on giving to the other person that we don't allow ourselves to acknowledge what we are receiving, the ecstasy of orgasm will not wash over us. We must invite it.

> It is a paradox of lovemaking that we must fully give *and* fully receive.

This can be difficult for many people, especially women who have been enculturated to always be in the serving role. They may become highly aroused but repeatedly back off from climax because of discomfort with having the focus entirely on themselves. Men who experience delayed ejaculation sometimes evidence this same hesitancy to receive. If you have ever had a loved one not know how to gratefully receive a Christmas gift, you can understand that it is no sign of love to refuse a spouse's gift of sexual pleasure. It is a paradox of lovemaking that we must fully give *and* fully receive, just as we must fully give ourselves to God *and* fully receive the gift of himself. Then, and only then, do we become one.

The couple who is able to be playfully vulnerable, mutually exploring each other's body, soul, and spirit, and who can flood with the sensory cues of lovemaking and allow their passion to build is ready to spill down into the third quadrant of our model, the Apex. This is the consummation of the act of two becoming one.

Questions for Couples

- In what ways could you and your spouse create a more playful spirit in the bedroom?

- Are there ways in which you could become more exploratory with your spouse physically, mentally, emotionally, and spiritually?

- List your sensual turn-ons and turnoffs, as explained in the chapter. Are there ways you could expand the ones that cause arousal? Are there any turnoffs you could eliminate?

- Do you need to become more comfortable receiving sexual pleasure? If so, are you resolved to doing so?

8

Apex

The Point of Surrender

If a woman does not obtain natural gratification from the sexual act there is a danger that her experience of it will be qualitatively inferior, will not involve her fully as a person. This sort of experience makes nervous reactions only too likely, and may for instance cause secondary sexual frigidity. Frigidity is sometimes the result of an inhibition on the part of the woman herself, or of a lack of involvement which may even at times be her own fault. But it is usually the result of egoism in the man, who failing to recognize the subjective desires of the woman in intercourse, and the objective laws of the sexual process taking place in her, seeks merely his own satisfaction, sometimes quite brutally.

Pope John Paul II

Frank and Donna were referred by Frank's oncologist roughly four months after he underwent surgery for prostate cancer. They were in their late fifties, empty nesters, pleasant and friendly in a reserved sort of way.

113

As I greeted them in our lobby, I sensed an apathy or hopelessness in their spirit and demeanor. We opened in prayer and Frank began. "I'll be real honest with you, Chris. I'm not sure you can do much to help us. As you know, I've had prostate surgery. The doctor told us it would be some time before I'd regain urinary continence and erectile function. He also told us that some men never really get those back and they just have to live with the equipment not working right. I guess I'm one of those guys. I'm doing better with the continence, but I can't get much of an erection and, even when I do, I often don't climax. It's pretty well killed our sex life, but I don't see what talking to you is going to do about that—no offense."

I met them in their grief and acknowledged that I could scarcely imagine all they had gone through over the past several months. However, I challenged them not to give up hope on their sexual intimacy so quickly. I gathered information about their presurgery sex life and details of patterns they had noticed since the operation, exploring when things seemed to work better and especially when they felt most connected to each other. Over the next several sessions we also discussed what sex had meant to each of them throughout their marriage.

It would be nice to report that Frank eventually regained complete control over his erections and ejaculation, but that is not the case. In fact far more men than we would imagine experience impairment or loss of these functions due to prostate problems, vascular (blood flow) problems, nerve damage, complications from diabetes or other disorders, medication side effects, and other factors. *But this does not need to spell the end for a rich and satisfying sex life.* Frank and Donna discovered that their enjoyment of connecting with each other and talking, teasing, and massaging each other while undressed actually *increased* when they stopped focusing so much on just completing the act of intercourse.

Their level of transparency with each other also increased as they were willing to try various means of aiding Frank's erections, such as a prescription vacuum pump[1] and Viagra. Frank came to a greater understanding of what Donna had said throughout their years together about her enjoyment of being one with him even if orgasm didn't occur. They found that they actually became more comfortable with nudity and with prolonging sex play than they had ever experienced in their marriage.

"It's like sex for us now is about so much more than just me climaxing inside her," Frank said in one of our final sessions. "Sometimes it happens and sometimes it doesn't, but we're so much more present or intimate with each other than I remember before. I feel like I know Donna more deeply and like I understand now what she's always said she enjoyed about sex. I understand what you've been saying, about the difference between 'having sex' and 'making love.'"

Donna laughed and confirmed, "Frank makes love to me better now than he ever did before the operation!"

This kind of growth happened because Frank and Donna were willing to talk, and keep on talking, even when they didn't feel there was much point. They loved each other and their marriage enough not to let sexual intimacy die when things were no longer as they had always been.

"It would have been easier to just let it go and accept it as one more sign of growing old, like my hair falling out or my love handles," said Frank. "I didn't want to talk about something I didn't feel I could do anything about."

Donna added, "But I think we would have become like so many other couples we see who don't even hold hands anymore. You know they haven't been sexual in years. Frank is actually more tender and attentive toward me now than he's ever been, and I think a lot of it has to do with us broadening our enjoyment of each other sexually."

Making love is about so much more than intercourse and orgasms. God has designed orgasms as an important part of lovemaking, and they are certainly to be desired and pursued by both partners when the body is capable of producing them, but making them the only focus greatly limits lovemaking. Couples who are principally chasing orgasms never get past simply having sex and are therefore constantly looking for something new to stimulate and give them a bigger and better climax. (This desire is the only thing keeping many men's and women's magazines in business!)

> **A woman's orgasm is much more complex than a man's.**

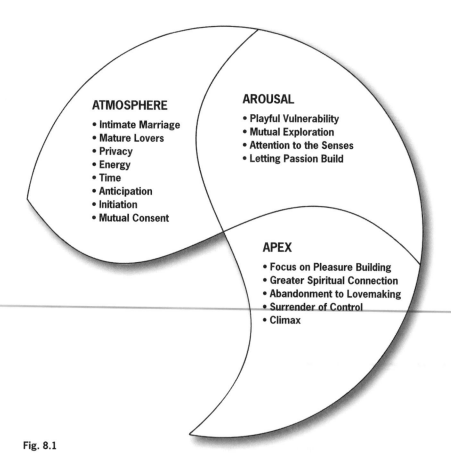

ATMOSPHERE

• Intimate Marriage
• Mature Lovers
• Privacy
• Energy
• Time
• Anticipation
• Initiation
• Mutual Consent

AROUSAL

• Playful Vulnerability
• Mutual Exploration
• Attention to the Senses
• Letting Passion Build

APEX

• Focus on Pleasure Building
• Greater Spiritual Connection
• Abandonment to Lovemaking
• Surrender of Control
• Climax

Fig. 8.1

By the same token, climaxing mustn't be minimized either, especially for the woman. Unless a man has some kind of physiological problem, he rarely thinks, *I wonder if I'll have an orgasm this time.* It's a forgone conclusion—it will almost surely happen. But many women, perhaps the majority, wonder, *Will I have an orgasm this time?* A woman's orgasm is much more complex than a man's.

> **Orgasm will not occur without an active invitation to flood one's awareness with the enjoyment of sexual stimulation.**

As couples allow passion to build in the Arousal phase, it will eventually enable them to spill into the third quadrant of our model, the Apex. Note that this phase is not called "orgasm" as in Masters and Johnson's model, because it may not always result in that for one or both partners. We are not working for the big "mutual O." We are not even working for the woman to have an orgasm every time, although it should occur with good frequency. But if couples are joining together in body, soul, and spirit, there will come a point at which they feel most aware of that union with each other, and this will generally be marked by at least the man's orgasm. This is the Apex.

Focus on Pleasure Building

In 1998 Dr. Archibald Hart, Dr. Catherine Hart Weber, and sex therapist Debra Taylor published a landmark survey on the sexuality of more than two thousand evangelical Christian women from all walks of life.[2] Their findings showed that women who achieve orgasm at least 50 percent of the time were more sexually satisfied or fulfilled than those for whom orgasm occurred less than 25 percent of the time. Clearly there was a correlation between frequency of orgasm and satisfaction with lovemaking. However, their survey also found that *59 percent of the women were unable to reach orgasm by intercourse alone.* Some studies have reported this figure as high as 66 percent—two-thirds of all women. These figures underscore the point that orgasm is more complex for women than for men.

For climax to occur, each partner must begin to tune in to and focus on the pleasurable sensations beginning to build within his or her body. Both partners must give themselves permission to keep drinking in the mental, emotional, and physical pleasures of sexual arousal and to tune out all other distractions. Most men seem to do this quite easily—sometimes too easily, resulting in premature ejaculation. Women generally struggle more, and sometimes a woman's body will not cooperate well. This can be due to a particular stage in her cycle, perimenopausal or meno-pausal complications, or postpartum states. Certainly negative views toward sex or her body, conflict in the marriage, stress and fatigue, medication reactions, and a history of sexual abuse can greatly impair a woman's ability to have a positive response to pleasurable sensations. Even simply being mentally preoccupied will dampen arousal enough to impair it. Orgasm will not occur without an active invitation to flood one's awareness with the enjoyment of sexual stimulation.

One of the most important factors in a woman's achieving climax lies in sufficient and direct clitoral stimulation. In the Hart/Weber/Taylor study, more than 62 percent of the respon-dents said they required *fifteen minutes or more* of direct clitoral stimulation to achieve orgasm. Since studies have shown that most men are unable to withhold climax for more than two to five minutes during active thrusting, and most women do not receive direct clitoral stimulation during active thrusting, it is easy to understand why most women are unable to achieve orgasm through intercourse alone. Most will need manual stimulation of their clitoris before, during, or after intercourse to facilitate climax.

This emphasizes the importance of allowing sufficient time and energy for lovemaking. We have often heard women jokingly referred to as crock-pots and men as microwaves, but there is some real truth in the comparisons. Generally women require a much greater sense of closeness, emotional intimacy, affirmation, romance, and slow but deliberate buildup to allow an orgasm to wash over them. Thank goodness! These needs are the real lifeblood of making love. If women responded just like men, we might resemble two dogs in heat rather than Christ romancing his bride.

Men, be careful not to rush things and miss this emotional connecting. Prematurely climaxing will leave your wife feeling frustrated sexually and in every other way. This is one of those times when the principle of ladies first works especially well! Pay attention to her and allow her pleasure to build and even crest before turning to your own pleasure.

> **Men, be careful not to rush things.**

Focus more on the clitoris than the vaginal area—remember that God gave your wife a clitoris for the sole purpose of your being able to pleasure her to climax. Remember too that the clitoris is a densely packed bundle of nerve endings, making it highly sensitive—take your cues from her as to what feels good and how she wants to be touched. What felt good last time you made love may not feel good tonight, and what felt good two minutes ago may be irritating now. What a wonderful invitation God has given us to communicate more openly during lovemaking!

A final note on this: I have heard many women complain about God's design for the woman, feeling it is unfair that the man's nerve endings are distributed along the entire shaft of the penis while hers are so densely clustered in the tiny bundle of the clitoris, making it far more difficult to climax during actual intercourse. However, as my friend and colleague Dr. Bill Cutrer points out, childbirth would be unimaginably painful if those same nerve endings were distributed around the opening of the vagina. God has not neglected the woman's pleasure but equipped her for it without making childbirth unbearable. In this we see again God's twofold plan for sex—for procreation as well as for pleasure and bonding.

Greater Spiritual Connection

As a couple focuses on their pleasure and shuts out all other distractions, they enter a wonderful space of greater spiritual connection. They begin to lose a sense of where each ends and the other begins. They may feel temporarily suspended in time, unaware of anything else but what they are experiencing in that moment. As the wife invites the husband inside and they become one in body, they also become one in soul and spirit, being now fully naked physically, emotionally, and spiritually.

It is impossible to describe this state with words. All attempts fall short and sound hollow. As has been said, intercourse provides us a means of communicating with our bodies what our words cannot. We are *one* in marriage in the truest sense of that word, and our bodies are able to bear testimony to that oneness.

> We are *one* in marriage in the truest sense of that word, and our bodies are able to bear testimony to that oneness.

This bodily expression is a little like another function God gave us for communicating things deep inside of us—the act of crying. Why did God give us the capacity to cry? I don't know. I don't like to cry. But I know that when I am in great pain in my soul and spirit and I allow myself to cry, I describe it as "having a good cry." Why? Because it releases something inside of me. Something is communicated through my body to myself (and to anyone who cares and loves me) about the truth of my pain. Somehow, in giving expression to my pain through my tears, the power of that expression makes it more real and I am more able to integrate that truth into my being. My words could not express it; my tears do.

This is what the act of intercourse can do in Christian marriage when it is practiced within this broader scope of making love, as we have detailed. When we lose ourselves in the ecstasy of oneness with our Adam or our Eve, we bear witness to the truth of that oneness, and the power of its expression makes it more real to us. Not only so, but because he who is Truth is also present in our union, our covenant is renewed in the heavenlies. This is why we are not to refrain from sexual relations for long. Just as holy communion renews our covenant oneness with Christ, sexual union renews our covenant oneness with each other.

Abandonment to Lovemaking, Surrender of Control, and Climax

There comes a point, as pleasure builds and the two become one, at which we must abandon ourselves to each other and allow climax to wash over us. This occurs in a matter of mere seconds. At orgasm, we release control of the body and allow ecstasy to take over, creating involuntary muscle spasms throughout. Our central nervous system becomes flooded with endorphins and enkephalins, highly pleasurable and painkilling neurochemistry, which produce an indescribable feeling of euphoria. We become lost for a few precious moments together.

This is the point we call climax. Whether it includes orgasm on the part of both persons or is just a wonderful time of intimate connecting, this is the climax of sexual union. It cements us more strongly to each other, bonding us as nothing else can. We give all of ourselves, holding nothing back, and cling to each other as the power of our love is released through our bodies.

We have referred several times to bonding or pairing during sexual arousal and climax, and this is a critical point to understand. Our bodies pair many sensory cues during heightened states of arousal. We see this in victims of crime or in those who have been in war zones or survived natural disasters. During the threat, when their body experienced its fight or flight response, these people were rapidly taking in sensory cues from the environment to help them survive. Their heart rate and respiration greatly increased, and their vision, hearing, and other senses became keenly focused. The body tried to take in as much information as it could to protect itself. Afterward, those who survive such ordeals often find that various sensory cues trigger their central nervous system back into that fight or flight state. The sound of a gunshot or a helicopter overhead can put a war veteran into a state of high alert or panic. The smell of alcohol on someone's breath can cause a flashback in a rape victim whose abuser had been drunk. These are pictures of negative pairing.

In a much more positive way, our bodies pair all kinds of pleasurable sensory cues during states of heightened sexual arousal. As we become more and more excited, our central nervous system pulls in and records the many sensations being experienced—the sight of our spouse's face, body, and skin, the taste of his kiss, the touch of her hand, the sound of his voice, the smell of her perfume. We store these cues, largely unconsciously, and they bond us more and more strongly to each other, just as an infant bonds to its mother through her holding, feeding, caressing, and singing. There are few other times when we can bond so strongly to each other. This is why we say that fostering a vibrant and passionate love life is like pouring superglue all over your marriage.

Letting go, surrendering control, abandoning self, becoming one—are these not metaphors for the spiritual life? Much of our growth in intimacy with Christ involves letting go, giving him more and more control over our lives so that he becomes everything and we nothing. This is absolute surrender. There are surely many sexual metaphors for spiritual truths that we miss because of not having a well-developed theology of sex. God uses much more sexual metaphor than we may be comfortable with, and certainly more than we understand. Allow him to teach you and your spouse as you learn to give yourselves more and more completely to each other.

Questions for Couples

- Has an overemphasis on orgasm robbed the two of you of some of the enjoyment and intimacy God intends in your lovemaking?
- Is there anything you need to share with your partner that could enhance your mutual enjoyment of the Apex?
- Do the two of you need to give greater priority to the woman's pleasure and orgasm during lovemaking?
- Are there things you are beginning to understand more clearly about intimacy with God and each other because of your lovemaking?

9

Afterglow

Basking in Oneness

I have come into my garden, my sister, my bride;
   I have gathered my myrrh with my spice.
I have eaten my honeycomb and my honey;
   I have drunk my wine and my milk.

Eat, O friends, and drink;
   drink your fill, O lovers.

Song of Songs 5:1

When Tammy first discovered her husband, Steve, was frequenting strip joints and massage parlors and masturbating to material from the Internet, she felt that her whole world had blown up. This was a side of him she knew nothing about, and she realized she couldn't trust anything he said or did. They separated for a few days while she collected herself and scheduled their first session with me. They didn't tell anyone because of Steve's position as the music minister at their prominent community church. They reunited initially only for the sake of their three children.

Tammy was devastated, wondering what she had done wrong that her husband would look elsewhere for sexual fulfillment. Steve was a broken man, acknowledging that his addiction had nothing to do with Tammy but had been a part of him long before he met her. He expressed a sense of relief that the secret was out and that he no longer had to live his double life, but they both doubted that their marriage could be saved, and, if it could, neither believed they could ever truly heal and become intimate again.

That was more than three years ago. After an intensive out-of-state program for Christian men with sexual addictions, weekly therapy group meetings in my practice, and individual or couples sessions on a weekly or biweekly basis, they had made tremendous progress. Steve had come to understand how he paired self-nurture with masturbation to pornography when he was still a teenager in his broken, alcoholic home. Some of his first magazines had belonged to his stepfather, who left them lying around the house. Sex had become a means of escaping from his pain and loneliness, providing a fantasy world where he was loved and adored and where the high of an orgasm was the only pleasure he could ensure.

He saw how he had become a chameleon, a performer, always trying to be whoever people wanted him to be so they would like him. He saw that his musical talents had been used to draw praise and attention to himself, trying desperately to fill up the bottomless pit of self-loathing that was the result of not only his tragic childhood but the sexual sins he used to deaden his pain. And he saw that he had never viewed sex as anything other than a rush or a buzz; it was certainly not a means of sharing his soul, connecting with Tammy, expressing his love. It was most assuredly not a means of glorifying God.

Tammy too had grown through therapy, coming to realize that she had idolized Steve, looking up to him the way so many people in their congregation did, as if he could do no wrong. She had put him on a pedestal and had devoted her life to taking care of him, quickly jumping to his defense when anyone complained that he often didn't follow through on commitments and that he was more flash than substance. She had overlooked his inappropriate flirtations with women and had ignored her concerns when he came home late or when he didn't account for the money he spent.

They had grown as a couple as well as individuals, and there were no longer any secrets between them. Steve often marveled at how good it felt to be clean—with Tammy and with God. They had both done a great deal of confessing and forgiving. Voluntarily Steve had stepped down from his ministry position, confessing privately to his pastor and trusted leaders and taking a job at a local business. His focus had begun to shift from self to his wife and kids, and some of the newer men in the therapy group were looking to him as a role model for their own healing process. After several months of sexual fasting in their marriage, Steve and Tammy had resumed relations and had recently begun to feel for the first time that they were really connecting.

"In these past several months I can actually say I feel like Steve is with me in sex," explained Tammy. "Once I understood how he had misused sex and that it was simply an escape for him, I knew why I had never felt like I could connect with him—like he was a million miles away. It was the most incredibly lonely feeling, like he was there but he wasn't, like it would have been less painful if he'd simply not been there at all."

"It's still a struggle," confessed Steve. "When my body starts to respond to Tammy, it's like I want to kick into autopilot and just zone out into a fantasy. I have to consciously make myself stay in the here and now and focus on her. It really helps if I keep my eyes open and look at her, talk to her, stay tuned in to her needs. I'm much less likely to zone out if we're talking."

There were definitely still times when they could tell Steve had fallen into his old patterns and was simply having sex rather than making love. Some nights they realized the best way they could make love was to simply fall asleep holding hands or lying in each other's arms. Other times they would interrupt lovemaking to talk or cry or pray for the Lord to keep healing them. They especially prayed that their children would never struggle with this problem—that the sins of the father would not be "handed down to the son" (Exod. 20:5). (We discussed in a session how the next verse in that passage states that God shows "love to a thousand generations of those who love him and keep his commandments." Instantly Steve responded: "I want to be the pivotal generation in my family line that makes that possible!")

"I've noticed something," Tammy observed in one of our sessions. "I can tell whether or not Steve has been with me in sex during those first few minutes after he's climaxed. It's like I can tell in my spirit whether we've really made love or just had sex. If we made love, I feel really close to him and have kind of a warm glowing feeling all over my body. Usually we lie there and snuggle for a few minutes, just soaking in that feeling.

"But if we just had sex, he seems distant from me, and I feel almost cold and alone—like I've been used or something. I don't cry anymore, like I used to, because I know it's not always going to be perfect. Sometimes I'm even the one who's not tuned in to him, because I was thinking about the kids or something. But I love it when we can both tell we really made love. There's no other feeling in the world like that."

It may be difficult to imagine ever healing from something as painful as what Tammy and Steve faced, but I have walked with numerous couples through that process. Although God would never have wanted them to struggle with such brokenness, he is able to use all things for good for those who love him, just as his Word promises. The marriages that emerge from sexual-addiction recovery are actually more mature and intimate than the marriage of the average couple, because the pain of their battle has driven them to each other and to a deeper relationship with God. If your

The Lovemaking Cycle

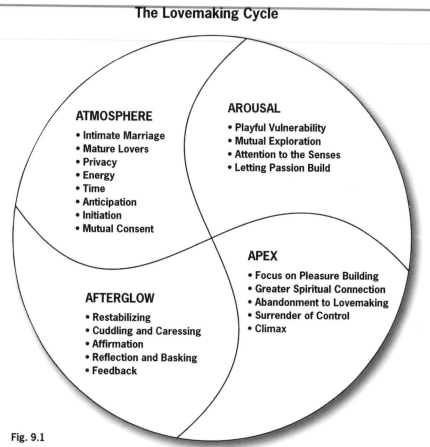

ATMOSPHERE
- Intimate Marriage
- Mature Lovers
- Privacy
- Energy
- Time
- Anticipation
- Initiation
- Mutual Consent

AROUSAL
- Playful Vulnerability
- Mutual Exploration
- Attention to the Senses
- Letting Passion Build

APEX
- Focus on Pleasure Building
- Greater Spiritual Connection
- Abandonment to Lovemaking
- Surrender of Control
- Climax

AFTERGLOW
- Restabilizing
- Cuddling and Caressing
- Affirmation
- Reflection and Basking
- Feedback

Fig. 9.1

© 1998 Christopher W. McCluskey, MSW

marriage is marred by sexual addiction or sexual sins, answer that challenge and seek out the help that is available.

The feeling of closeness and intimacy Tammy described after making love occurs in what I have called the Afterglow phase. This is a time of collecting ourselves and basking in what has just occurred. It is generally the briefest of the four quadrants in our model, often only a few minutes, but, as Tammy pointed out, it is the point at which we can most easily discern the spirit of the act in which we have just engaged.

Restabilizing

The first element of Afterglow is a period of restabilizing. This is a point at which you may feel most aware of how naked you really are. You have just surrendered yourself to your partner and allowed your central nervous system to take control of your body. You may have groaned or squealed or laughed or cried. In a state of physical, emotional, and spiritual ecstasy, you have been as vulnerable with each other as two humans can be. And now your bodies are no longer carrying you along in that highly aroused state. You may feel immediately self-conscious, awed but also embarrassed at how much you let go and how incredible it felt. You may feel the need to collect yourself and regain some sense of composure.

> **Rather than focusing on your own sudden self-consciousness, plug into the vulnerability of your spouse and heap praises on him or her.**

It may be tempting to pull away and reestablish yourself, perhaps by jumping out of bed to clean up. But in this precious window of time, you can choose instead to linger in the moment, cementing an awareness of the bond you just sealed. Rather than focusing on your own sudden self-consciousness, plug into the vulnerability of your spouse and heap praises on him or her. Remember that vulnerability means risk. Your husband or wife has just taken a risk, hoping you'll be pleased with him or her as a lover and that you're glad the two of you are one. Confirm the love you just expressed by verbally saying, "I love you!" This is like the amen at the end of an impassioned prayer. It emphasizes how sincerely you meant what your bodies just said.

This is critically important. In these awkward few moments of pulling yourselves back together, a few loving words and the willingness to tarry in each other's arms reinforce the bonding discussed in the previous chapter. It's like giving the glue time to set up. There are few other times when praise means so much or when criticism can hurt so deeply. Be very careful how you handle these precious moments.

Cuddling, Caressing, and Affirmation

Return to the metaphor of a Thanksgiving feast we considered in chapter 7. I cringe when I hear of families pushing back from the table immediately after sharing Thanksgiving dinner and saying, "Well, let's go watch the game!" Ugh! They are missing half the fun! It is so much more enjoyable to kick back and say, "Ohhh man, Aunt Marna, I don't know how you do it, but every year that pie gets better! Uncle Phil, way to go on that turkey! And, Grandma, I don't know what we'd do without your stuffing and gravy!" As you soak in that satiated feeling in your belly and soul, you praise each other and enjoy the time together. Nibbling on a little of this and a little of that—you are basking! You are taking in and storing up what was just shared. That is the spirit of Afterglow.

> **When a couple chooses to remain in the moment, cuddling, caressing, and affirming each other, they are storing up material to reflect on the next time they anticipate making love.**

Immediately after climax, you may feel the need to do some initial cleanup, and that is okay, but don't let it become a distraction. Keep some tissues by the bed and return to each other's arms as quickly as possible. Cuddle and kiss, drinking in the joy of being together. Caress each other's skin, stroke each other's hair, and gaze into each other's eyes, verbally sharing what is in your heart.

Notice how this feeds into the rest of our Lovemaking Cycle. When a couple chooses to remain in the moment, cuddling, caressing, and affirming each other, they are storing up material to reflect on the next time they anticipate making love. I have heard many clients say, "I wish I could remember how wonderful it feels right after we've made love—maybe we wouldn't wait so long between times!"

Reflection, Basking, and Feedback

Whenever I teach on Afterglow, I always think of my college roommate's pet cockatiels. He had a male and a female, and these birds had sexual relations all the time—they were very happy cockatiels. (When you're a single in college, this is *really* annoying.) But each time they finished mating, they would spend several minutes cooing and rubbing their heads against each other. It was as if they were expressing how much they loved each other—maybe that's why they had relations so often!

Be playful in sharing, careful not to criticize, but daring to be really honest.

That is a picture of Afterglow. It is letting each other know "I am so glad I'm married to you. You are such a tremendous lover. I love you so much." It says, "That was incredible! What did you do that time?" or "Well, that didn't work so well, did it? That's okay, honey, I still love being with you." It is affirming and praising and celebrating your oneness.

Providing each other with honest feedback is important for letting each other know what felt good and what didn't, what you loved and what you'd like to add or change next time. This is a way to build your repertoire of things that turn you on and to keep working on the things that turn you off. Remember, you are adding ways to build bonds between you. Be playful in sharing, careful not to criticize but daring to be really honest. Don't expect your spouse to read your mind and then become resentful when he or she can't. The two of you will grow in your ability to connect as one if you keep talking and risking, refusing to passively settle for the same old patterns year after year.

Bask in these moments together. For whatever reason, it is often difficult to linger in a wonderful moment. We are so driven by goals and the completion of tasks that just *being* feels awkward and unfamiliar. We would all do well to learn how to soak up our loved ones more at the holidays, to savor the feeling of our children nestled asleep in our arms, or to drink in the beauty of the night sky on a romantic moonlit walk. Afterglow is a time for practicing such skills. It can even deepen your ability to connect with God during times of private meditation. Only by learning to luxuriate in the present and becoming more fully aware of God in all things—especially in our oneness—can we experience much of the joy of the Christian life.

Questions for Couples

- ❧ How do you typically feel immediately after making love? Think of several words to describe your emotions during this time of collecting yourself.

- ❧ What messages have you given your spouse, whether verbally or nonverbally, during this brief period?

- ❧ What messages have you received from your spouse, whether verbally or nonverbally?

- ❧ In what ways could the two of you improve your ability to connect more deeply in the Afterglow?

Part 3

DIRECT
APPLICATION

10

Questions Men Ask

Do not merely listen to the word, and so deceive yourselves. Do what it says. Anyone who listens to the word but does not do what it says is like a man who looks at his face in a mirror and, after looking at himself, goes away and immediately forgets what he looks like. But the man who looks intently into the perfect law that gives freedom, and continues to do this, not forgetting what he has heard, but doing it—he will be blessed in what he does.

James 1:22–25

I love speaking to Christians on God's plan for sexuality. The topic never fails to draw a crowd and the energy in the room is palpable; people are so hungry for answers. But when I ask if there are any questions, most audiences fall dead silent. Understandably, very few people are bold enough to ask questions about sex in a room full of people, especially in church! So several years ago I began handing out 3 x 5 index cards and asking people to write down any questions they have. The cards are collected and I read them aloud and respond. It proves to be a very effective way to expand on the material and help couples apply it directly to their unique struggles. Otherwise, we run the risk of gaining insights but not changing behaviors.

It would be impossible to list all of the questions I've received through the years, but there are several that, in one form or another, seem to come up frequently. We have chosen twelve of these that men ask, and an equal number that women ask, which we will address in the next chapter. This is to assist in integrating the theological concepts of the first section of this book with the schematic model of the second. Hopefully you'll see pieces of your marriage in several of these questions. We encourage you to read all of them in sequence, even if they do not at first appear to apply to you—each may help establish a clearer picture of the spirit of making love.

My wife and I have been married nine years and our sex life has become extremely predictable and almost boring. It's like we're following a script we memorized years ago. I know I shouldn't introduce pornography, but how else can I liven things up?

You are certainly correct about not introducing pornography—few things are more damaging than that, in spite of what the "sexperts" may say. Introducing porn is a literal invitation for Satan to join you in bed. Unfortunately, many Christians do exactly that, if not through pornography then by watching steamy R-rated movies together, reading graphic sex scenes from popular best-sellers, or fantasizing about their favorite movie stars.

> **Preventing predictability and boredom requires attention, forethought, and creativity.**

To be sure, these activities will bring a new rush to sexual arousal, but they are absolute *poison* to the intimate connecting of true lovemaking.

Preventing predictability and boredom requires attention, fore-thought, and creativity. Recall the analogy of Thanksgiving dinner. A memorable Thanksgiving dinner is so much more than a prebaked turkey from Wal-Mart, Stove-Top stuffing, and a Sara Lee pie. Those may be the right foods, but they speak of little to no planning, preparation, or effort. They don't create a magical, connecting, celebratory atmosphere. They simply get the job done. It's easy to let our sex lives become something we treat like a microwave meal, but, when we do, we don't realize what we are forfeiting.

The art of creating a true Thanksgiving Day feast requires plan-ning; coordination; investment of time and money; attention to decorating and mood setting; stimulation of the senses through candlelight, rich aromas, music, and the like; creativity in food preparation and presentation; rituals to facilitate conversation and laughter; and allowance of ample time for guests to relax and enjoy each other without feeling rushed. Many people have *never* experienced a holiday meal like that. The Bible gives numerous accounts of Jewish feasts that routinely lasted several days to a week. That requires serious planning and effort! If Jewish love-making was anything like their feasting, they were enjoying each other much more like the lovers in the Song of Songs than like many modern-day Christians.

When lovemaking lacks anticipation, preparation, and creative initiation, it becomes boring. Don't settle for sexual fast food. It's better to decrease the frequency of sexual relations and increase the investment in feasting when you do come together. Commit to luxuriating together. Do the five-senses exercise described in chapter 7 and commit to enhancing your sensuality. Introduce new things to increase your vulnerability while also pleasuring each other with the things you've enjoyed for years. "The mandrakes send out their fragrance, and at our door is every delicacy, *both new and old,* that I have stored up for you, my lover" (Song 7:13, emphasis added). *Plan* sensual feasts.

I like to be spontaneous, but my wife keeps insisting that she needs time to prepare for sex. Planning everything out ahead of time takes a lot of the fun out of it for me. Shouldn't lovemaking be about letting ourselves get caught up in the heat of the moment and just going with it?

Certainly there are times when it's important to seize the moment and let your passions run wild. Sex should never become so planned and scheduled that there's no room for spontaneity, but, as we discussed in chapter 7, men are generally much more responsive to a few subtle cues and a little friction than are women. If you want your wife to give herself to you passionately, align yourself with the way her sexuality works and give her more time and reason to anticipate and prepare herself. Romance her and increase her desire—don't just try to get her turned on. The more aware she is of your love, your sensitivity to her needs and desires, and that you want more than just a fix, the more she will want to give herself to you. This greater interest in giving herself to you will probably result in a little more spontaneity in her as well.

Sometimes the main reason I want to be sexual is simply for release from sexual tension. Like Paul says in 1 Corinthians 7:9, "It is better to marry than to burn with passion." My wife complains of feeling used when I feel like that, but isn't this a biblical principle for marriage?

There is no question that one of the blessings of marriage is having a God-honoring outlet for sexual tension. But this is a very delicate issue and one that cuts right to the heart of Jesus' insistence on discerning the spirit of the law and not looking only at the letter of the law. If the *primary* spirit behind a sexual encounter is the release of the man's sexual tension and if the wife feels used, then the act is neither God-honoring nor good for the marriage. "'Everything is permissible for me'—but not everything is beneficial. 'Everything is permissible for me'—but I will not be mastered by anything" (1 Cor. 6:12). Don't exercise your "rights within the law" at the cost of your wife feeling used. You can easily become mastered by your sexual desires, even within marriage. Freedom must always be balanced with self-control. It's hard to imagine God being pleased and honored by an act that leaves your wife feeling used, however lawful the act may be. Turn your desire for sex into a greater ability to make love to your wife in nonsexual ways by spending time together, talking, doing shared activities, and serving her. You'll have a stronger marriage, and she'll be more likely to *want* to be sexual with you.

My wife seems hypersensitive to touch. She always complains that my touch tickles, irritates, or hurts her. How can we make love when I can't even touch her?

This is actually a fairly common complaint, and it is usually indicative of the body not having been adequately aroused prior to being touched in very sensitive regions. Recall that in chapter 4 we detailed the body's erogenous zones and emphasized focusing first on level three zones with handholding, hugs, gentle back rubs, and stroking arms and shoulders, gradually progressing to the level two zones of neck, face, temples, head, small of the back, abdomen, backs of the legs, and inner thighs. Intersperse your touch with tender kisses, waiting for her response before becoming more passionate, eventually exploring her neck, ear lobes, shoulders, and beyond with your lips and tongue. Taking this more gradual approach creates a buildup of sexual tension that makes her body *crave* the more erotic touch of level one zones, which, when touched only moments before, would have felt tickled or irritated.

The key is to start broadly, gradually becoming more specific and focused. Take your cues from her as to where she wants to be touched and when she wants more. Remember to talk and ask playful questions. Don't just guess and fumble along in frustrated silence. Allow her to begin rhythmically pressing in to your touch rather than creating all the pressure and friction yourself. Give her greater control over when, where, and how she wants to be touched and neither of you will likely continue to be frustrated by hypersensitivity.

My wife's sex drive is definitely less than mine, and one of the ways I deal with that is through masturbation. I won't say I feel good about it, but it seems more loving than pressuring her all the time, and the Bible doesn't specifically forbid it. What do you say about this?

Masturbation is one of the most volatile subjects that can be brought up in a talk on sex, and I am asked about it every time I speak. Christian opinion seems to run the gamut, from it never being acceptable for any reason to allowance for it under certain circumstances to great freedom with it as long as it is not coupled with fantasy about someone other than one's spouse. (Obviously if masturbation is coupled with fantasy about others, it is lust, which *is* specifically forbidden.[1])

We can all at least agree that masturbation is considerably less than God's full intention for sexuality and that, if we give in too easily to our sexual appetite, we can quickly become mastered by it. To those who feel masturbation is a lawful practice, I urge you to exercise vigilance in ensuring that it does not master you or foster laziness, robbing your marriage and spiritual life of the intimacy that is often found only in wrestling through temptations. To those couples who disagree on it, I urge you to press in for answers and keep a periodic dialogue going until you arrive at a position about

> **We can all at least agree that masturbation is considerably less than God's full intention for sexuality.**

which you both can feel peaceful. To those who feel it is never right under any circumstances, I urge you to ensure that you are operating on conviction—that you know *why* you believe as you do—and are not simply reacting out of your emotions.

As we discussed in the first several chapters, sexuality is principally about relationship and love—a means by which we can give ourselves completely and only to another and can receive a complete self-donation in return, confirming our oneness in spirit. C. S. Lewis captured this well in his response to a young man about masturbation:

> For me the real evil of masturbation would be that it takes an appetite which, in lawful use, leads the individual out of himself to complete his own personality in that of another and turns it back; sends the man back into the prison of himself, there to keep a harem of imaginary brides.
>
> And this harem, once admitted, works against his ever getting out and really uniting with a real woman. For the harem is: always accessible, always subservient, calls for no sacrifices or adjustments, and can be endowed with erotic and psychological attractions which no real woman can rival. Among those shadowy brides he is: always adored, always the perfect love, no demand is made of his unselfishness, no mortification ever imposed on his vanity. In the end, they become merely the medium through which he increasingly adores himself.[2]

This threat to intimacy is present even for the man who fantasizes about his wife, since he is in complete control of how she responds in his mind. Again, I urge great caution if you and your spouse choose to allow for periodic masturbation.

I feel bombarded daily with sexual images through the media and our culture, let alone the stuff on the Internet. I know we are supposed to be "in the world but not of the world," but how is a man with a healthy libido supposed to deal with these constant temptations?

If you are feeling bombarded by sexual images in the media and the culture, it's because you *are* being bombarded! The sexual revolution has had sweeping victories and the counterculture of the '60s has become today's culture. Our once fairly conservative, quasi-Christian American culture has become the subculture. We have become like Lot, living in a modern-day Sodom. As we said in chapter 1, we face daily temptations through the media that no previous culture has ever faced. One of the many reasons Rachel and I moved from Tampa Bay to our family's ranch in rural Missouri was to get away from the constantly increasing number of adult video stores and bookstores, peep shows, strip joints, lingerie "modeling" parlors, and the like. However, in the five years we've lived here, we have seen an adult video store come to the town immediately to our north and there are strip joints within a half-hour's drive.

We can't live in a box and, even if we were to move far away to some other country in an effort to protect ourselves and our families, we would be unable to escape the presence and influence of graphic sexual temptations. Through the media and the Internet, the world has become a very small place, and we have thoroughly polluted it with our distortions of God's beautiful gift. We have become like the great prostitute in Revelation, pumping our pornography and notions of free love and sex without consequences into every corner of the globe. The best we can do now is to be acutely aware of the danger and take appropriate measures to avoid it wherever possible. We cannot handle sexual temptations by trying to pretend they're not there or by thinking we are somehow above them. As Jesus instructed, we must be as shrewd as serpents and yet remain as innocent as doves (Matt. 10:16).

Be aware of when and where you are most vulnerable and then establish hedges and accountability wherever necessary. Consider changing the route you drive to work if it takes you past a place of constant temptation. Program your cable TV service to block stations that are problematic, and don't watch TV late at night or in rooms where you have absolute privacy. Install filtering software on your computer or contract with a porn-filtering Internet service.

> **Be aware of when and where you are most vulnerable and then establish hedges and accountability wherever necessary.**

Avoid men's magazines such as *GQ, Men's Health,* and others that promote the "*Playboy* ethic," even though they're not pornography per se. Be careful with the sports section of the newspaper where most providers of sex-oriented services advertise. Be diligent in monitoring what comes into your home, including catalogs such as *Victoria's Secret* and the magazines your children read.

Be honest with your wife and closest friends about areas in which you face particular temptation and ask them to be praying for you as well as asking you the hard questions for accountability. Stay connected to God. Remember, no matter what temptations you face, you are more than a conqueror *in Christ* (see Rom. 8:37).

A lot of things I do to get my wife aroused end up backfiring on me. I try letting her know I'm in the mood ahead of time with some sexy talk or taking my shirt off or wearing sexy underwear, but she usually turns off instead of getting turned on. I'm no Adonis, but I'm not unattractive and I know she loves me, so what am I missing?

This is a more complex question than it may seem at first because of the huge number of things that can affect sexual desire.

However, barring relational problems, medical or hormonal concerns, medication reactions, pain disorders, past trauma, stress and fatigue, and other factors (whew!), it may simply be that you are trying to entice her too much through overtly sexual cues, which a man desires, rather than through more relational, playful, romantic cues that invite her to slowly warm up to the idea of making love.

Rather than trying to guess what will turn your wife on, ask her—and then listen very closely! She may not be especially aware at first, but have the conversation often, inside and outside of the bedroom, and expand your repertoire over time. Some of your cues may actually be scaring her a bit; they may feel too racy or aggressive, and she may not feel she'll have as much control as she wants. Many wives complain that their husbands become like animals when they're revved up. Make a lifelong study of your wife—become an expert on her feminine spirit and her sexual triggers and learn to romance and pleasure her as no other man could.

I've never been a very macho guy and I understand what you're saying about the importance of embracing our masculinity, but I am never going to be the Marlboro man. I would love to image God more through my masculinity, but frankly I don't know how I can do that.

Remember that masculinity has more to do with inner character than outer physique. Some of the most shallow, immature, ungodly men I know have the outward physique of a Marlboro man. The Bible indicates that Jesus was not a particularly striking man; there was nothing about his natural appearance that would have drawn people to him. What drew people was his love and gentleness coupled with his strength of character. We are to reflect the same character. We are to become more and more like

Jesus, developing the mind of Christ, growing in his likeness, disciplining our flesh, and surrendering our lives daily so that he becomes everything and we nothing.

The inner strength of a Christian man, made in the image of God, is godly character wrought in the furnace of a surrendered, disciplined life. Read some of the many excellent Christian books on authentic manhood, such as *Tender Warrior* by Stu Weber or *Wild at Heart* by John Eldredge. Read books on developing godly character, such as *Like a Rock* by Andy Stanley or *The Quest for Character* by Chuck Swindoll. Go to some Christian conferences or retreats on authentic manhood.

It's important to attend to the outer man as well, as we emphasized in chapter 4. Remember that our bodies are the temple of the Holy Spirit and we are responsible for maintaining that temple. Pay attention to your grooming habits, hygiene, posture, and social skills. Develop good health practices—proper diet, good exercise, adequate sleep, and good stress management. Attend to your wardrobe and be conscious of how you are dressing. Very few of us will have a model's body and all of us will grow old, but we are responsible for investing what God has entrusted to us and bringing him a return on it, just as in the parable of the talents. Even if you feel like the man with one talent when it comes to your outer physique, be sure you don't neglect what God has given you. "Offer your bodies as living sacrifices, holy and pleasing to God—this is your spiritual act of worship" (Rom. 12:1).

I was present at the delivery of our baby, and I wouldn't trade that experience for anything, but seeing the baby born and especially watching the doctor perform an unexpected episiotomy have really messed up the way I feel about my wife's vagina. Any suggestions?

Join the crowd! Many men complain that, once their wives become pregnant, they have a difficult time maintaining sexual arousal in the face of all the changes in her body. Seeing our child pass through the birth canal and enter the world is the most amazing miracle any of us will ever witness, yet it's a difficult image to get out of our mind when trying to resume sexual relations.

Watching your wife's beautiful breasts become two large milk jugs can make it hard to keep them paired with arousal, especially when she has a letdown as you touch them. Her graceful legs can become riddled with varicose veins and her shapely hips covered with stretch marks. Her tummy will likely never be as firm as it was before pregnancy and may be scarred from a cesarean delivery. Many women develop trouble with urinary continence and sphincter control, and even when aggressive efforts are made to lose the weight and get the body back in shape, there will never again be the firmness of her virgin breasts and the tautness of her youthful skin. Even the man who lovingly praises his wife for sacrificing her body and who affirms the beauty of motherhood still experiences some degree of grief over the changes in her body (as does the woman).

> Even the man who lovingly praises his wife for sacrificing her body and who affirms the beauty of motherhood still experiences some degree of grief over the changes in her body (as does the woman).

Recall our discussion of sexual pairing (see chapter 7)—how various sensate stimuli can become paired with either arousal or aversion, and how people can often re-pair things that used to be turnoffs and make them turn-ons. I will not suggest that any of the things just mentioned can somehow be re-paired and become an erotic turn-on for you. (If we succeeded in that, we would probably have created some weird new fetish or something.) But though they may not get your sexual motor going, they can certainly draw you more to your wife in genuine love, respect, and admiration for the sacrifices she made to birth God's children. As you hold her body and caress her skin, be mindful of how fragile life is, how easily you could have lost her in childbirth, and how blessed you are to have her. Rehearse these awarenesses out loud, telling her how you feel. Use this as an opportunity to move beyond a primary focus on her physical body to learning instead to view her more fully as body, soul, and spirit. Tell her frequently how proud you are of her and let her "battle scars" draw your admiration as for a war hero. Though her bodily changes will not turn you on directly, they can deepen your relational love, which is far more arousing than any body could ever be.

You can also minimize or extinguish some of the powerful negative pairing that occurs, as in the episiotomy mentioned here. To a large degree, we can choose what we will focus on and what we'll ignore. As we accept what is or what has happened and actively grieve it—praying about it, journaling, and talking with appropriate people—we can move past negative occurrences and become more mature in the process. When, instead, we try to fight it, ignore it, or pretend it didn't happen or doesn't bother us, we can become stuck psychologically and develop an obsession with something that was disturbing. Accept what happened, pray about it, feel your feelings, grieve it, and move on. If it is helpful, try turning the image in your mind from full color to black and white, and try shrinking the image down to a tiny speck very far off in the distance. It then remains a part of your reality but has been consciously reduced to a tiny piece rather than an overwhelming obstacle.

My wife was sexually abused as a girl. We talked about it before getting married and we agreed to take things slowly, knowing sex might be difficult for us. However, it's been three years now and she still has an extremely hard time even disrobing in front of me, let alone having intercourse. I am not upset with her and I try to be very understanding, but I want to help and nothing is working. What should we do?

Time to get some help. Quite simply, when things have not improved over this amount of time, not only are you dealing with something that is fairly entrenched, but you may both be unwittingly reinforcing some of her fear-based reactions by trying to press on. Just as you don't "play through the pain" when there is physical pain during intercourse, you mustn't "just do it" when there are strong indications of emotional pain from sexual abuse. Not only can it create significant frustration and tension for both partners, but it can cause major marital rifts if the husband begins to become associated in the wife's mind with her abuser, or if the wife becomes increasingly angry with herself.

Seek out a skilled, licensed Christian therapist who specializes in work with sexual abuse and commit to the process until real healing is experienced. You may be able to locate one in your area through your pastor or through the American Board of Christian Sex Therapists (www.sexualwholeness.com). This may take a few years and may involve work with a therapy group in addition to one-on-one and couples counseling, but the time, energy, money, and pain invested bring indescribable rewards. Real, godly healing from sexual abuse produces profound changes in the person and in his or her marriage, family, and spiritual life.

I am forty-nine years old and my body is beginning to show some signs of the years—less muscle tone, more sags, some wrinkles, and a few extra pounds—but I can live with these. What has me concerned is occasional difficulty with erections and sometimes with ejaculation. Should I try medications?

Definitely not—at least not until you've ruled out some things. As men age, their ability to get and maintain an erection begins to decline; it's a natural part of the aging process. Additionally, the firmness of erections decreases as does the strength of ejaculations, and there is an increase in the amount of time needed after ejaculation before the body can produce another (called the refractory time). The felt need for ejaculation generally becomes less strong and the libido or overall sex drive may decline. These are *normal* results of the aging process, and, although not something we're thrilled about, they are nothing to become particularly concerned about. Each becomes more problematic, however, as a man begins to worry about and obsess over it, increasing his anxiety with each encounter in which things don't go as they used to.

> **A gradual decline in the overall intensity of your functioning can become an invitation to expand your definition of lovemaking.**

Many things can worsen these natural changes, and you should address as many of them as possible. These include emotional stress, smoking, excessive consumption of alcohol, drug usage (prescription and nonprescription as well as street drugs), prostate problems, diabetes, high or low blood pressure, nerve damage, decreased testosterone levels, and other medical problems.

Discuss significant changes in sexual functioning with your doctor, as there are many options for addressing problems. I am thankful that we have Viagra and other medications, but don't jump too quickly to them. A gradual decline in the overall intensity of your functioning can become an invitation to expand your definition of lovemaking beyond simply having intercourse and may enable you to slow down and connect more as a couple during prolonged times of foreplay. If you don't become overly focused on performance and instead enjoy a greater awareness of your love for your wife, lovemaking can take on a new depth of experience, even when things don't work quite right or when it requires more focus on sensuality and quality.

I struggle with pornography, fantasy, and masturbation. I've tried everything to control myself—rededicating my life, account-ability partners, Scripture memorization, pouring my energy into working out, even taking cold showers! I still keep falling time after time and I'm losing hope. What more can I do?

What you are describing is sexual addiction, and hope and help are definitely available. Some people scoff at the idea of sex as an addiction, but we know that anything that is mood altering (and sex certainly qualifies!) can become an addiction. The natural high of sexual arousal and orgasm produces an incredible amount of mood-altering neurochemistry that is extremely reinforcing and can create an addiction as powerful as any street drug. Combine that with the fact that it's free, it's legal, it won't show up on drug tests, society encourages it, and "usage" often begins in childhood or early adolescence, and you begin to understand why people can become so hooked.

This is not to suggest that sexual addiction is not still a sin. It absolutely is, and, as we emphasized in chapter 1, Scripture says it can keep us from inheriting the kingdom (see 1 Cor. 6:9–10). But it is not a sin that most people find themselves able to break free from without help. An addiction of any type can be thought of as a besetting sin—one that seems to control us. Paul addresses this in Galatians 6:1 when he says, "Brothers, if someone is caught in a sin, you who are spiritual should restore him gently. But watch yourself, or you also may be tempted." That word *caught* means "wrapped up and ensnared in." When a Christian is wrapped up and ensnared in sexual sin, the church is instructed to minister to him or her through gentle restoration. This is restoration of their whole personhood, not simply eradication of their behavior. It takes time and there are no quick fixes, but there can be real and lasting healing.

Note that Paul also emphasized being careful in working with such sins because we can find ourselves pulled into the same sin. It is my opinion that recovery from sexual addiction, like recovery from sexual abuse, is best facilitated by trained, licensed Christian therapists. This does not preclude the use of lay counseling and support groups, but these should be used in conjunction with a skilled professional who coordinates and oversees the recovery process.

Several excellent books have come out in the last ten years or so detailing a Christian approach to sexual addiction. I would particularly recommend *Faithful and True* by Dr. Mark Laaser, *Breaking Free* by Russell Willingham, *False Intimacy* by Dr. Harry Schaumburg, and *The Bondage Breaker* by Neal Anderson. Dr. Laaser and others also facilitate intensive retreats for men with sexual addictions. These resources are not a substitute for therapy, however, and should be used only in conjunction with a skilled Christian clinician. Be encouraged—those who wrestle through recovery from sexual addiction emerge at the other end as radically transformed men, husbands, fathers, and warriors in the King's army.

Questions for Couples

❧ What additional questions would you ask if given the opportunity right now?

- Are there any questions answered here that you need to discuss further as a couple?
- What actions do you need to take to address any of these issues?
- What do you feel is the number one male issue with sex in your marriage right now? What are you committed to doing about it?

11

Questions Women Ask

I am a wall,
   and my breasts are like towers.
Thus I have become in his eyes
   like one bringing contentment.
Solomon had a vineyard in Baal Hamon;
   he let out his vineyard to tenants.
Each was to bring for its fruit
   a thousand shekels of silver.
But my own vineyard is mine to give;
   the thousand shekels are for you, O Solomon.

Song of Songs 8:10–12

Dr. Joe McIlhaney is an obstetrician/gynecologist who frequently appears on Christian radio addressing issues of sexuality. He wrote the outstanding book *1250 Health-Care Questions Women Ask*. As I teased Rachel, that's a whole lot more questions than men ask! Women might counter that the only things men ask are "What's for dinner?" "Where's the remote?" and "Are you in the mood tonight?" That may be, but it does seem that women have a lot more questions about sex than men, and perhaps that's because sex is so much more complicated for women. There are

153

so many physiological issues, such as menstruation, discharges, infections, hormones, mood swings, pregnancy, delivery, nursing, and menopause, in addition to the greater emotional, relational, and spiritual awareness women bring to relations.

This book is principally about the spirit of lovemaking and not so much about the technical, physiological aspects. For that reason, we have selected twelve questions women ask that have to do with the emotional and relational side of things. There are several excellent Christian books that address physical concerns in great detail, most notably *A Celebration of Sex* by Dr. Doug Rosenau, *The Gift of Sex* by Dr. Clifford and Joyce Penner, *Sexual Intimacy in Marriage* by Dr. William Cutrer and Sandra Glahn, and *Intended for Pleasure* by Dr. Ed Wheat. The theology of these authors may differ from ours at points, but we can recommend any of these books if you are struggling with specific physiological problems. In addition, the book *Secrets of Eve: Understanding the Mystery of Female Sexuality* by Hart, Weber, and Taylor provides detailed information about the responses given by two thousand evangelical Christian women on a one-hundred-question survey about their sexuality. It provides an intimate look into the feelings and experiences of Christian women in the marital bedroom.

Following, then, are common questions I receive about the emotional and relational side of lovemaking. We hope you will see pieces of your marriage reflected here and that these will help flesh out a more complete picture of the spirit of making love.

Sex has been such a big disappointment. When we were dating, I used to think that since making out was so incredible, sex would be the ultimate. We've been married seven years now, and, although my husband seems to enjoy himself, I find our lovemaking quite unfulfilling. I've never shared this with him because he would take it very personally, like it's all his fault, but how can I be honest without hurting him?

I appreciate your sensitivity to your husband, but it may be that you'll be unable to broach this subject without some initial injury to his ego. It's imperative, however, that you bring it up. The reason is not simply because you're not fulfilled but because God has much more for both of you than you are currently experiencing and because the longer you go without being truthful about your feelings, the less honest, passionate, and intimate your lovemaking will become. If we could get enough distance and perspective to view your sex life across all the years you will share together, we would see that it is either drawing you closer together or moving you slowly apart. Problems often grow in silence and become firmly established with the passing of years.

You seem to recognize that the problem is not entirely your husband's fault; that's good. Although husbands are most often the initiators in marriage, this is not always the case, and, even when it is, they are still only half of the equation. Your piece for now—the piece you are responsible for before God—is simply to bring it up. Your husband may be entirely unaware that there is a problem.

Be as sensitive as you can and, ideally, bring it up outside of the bedroom; don't wait until you are just about to make love and then blurt it out. This is what often happens—the woman waits because of not wanting to hurt her husband's feelings and finally says something only when she is so aware of her own emotions that she can no longer remain silent. Not a particularly conducive setup for productive dialogue. The husband feels blindsided and becomes defensive; the wife misinterprets this as his not caring about how she feels; and they withdraw from each other with angry words or wounded silence.

Instead, be proactive and love your marriage enough to take the difficult step and bring it up when the two of you are relatively relaxed, when you are not distracted by television, the children, or other things, and when you have ample time to discuss it productively. Have some specific things in mind that you think may account for your dissatisfaction, and don't be too quick to drop the conversation if it becomes difficult. Be sure to cover the time in prayer. You are working hand in hand with God to make your marriage better. Don't surrender it to the enemy if things don't go particularly well at first.

> **Remember, fostering a healthy sex life is like pouring superglue all over your relationship!**

If your husband responds well, try reading together some of the books we've mentioned, or read sections of them to him if he's not a reader. Get a copy of the videotape pictured at the back of this book, *Coaching Couples into Passionate Intimacy.* It covers much of the material in this book with a detailed look at the Lovemaking Cycle model and may be easier for him to connect with than a book. If these don't help, consider a Christian therapist who specializes in sex therapy. There aren't many, but you may be able to locate one in your area through your pastor or through the American Board of Christian Sex Therapists (www.sexualwholeness.com). Even if you can't find a specialist, a good Christian counselor can help the two of you talk more productively and create a more mutually fulfilling experience. Remember, fostering a healthy sex life is like pouring superglue all over your relationship! That's worth working toward.

A premarital program we participated in said that men need to have sexual release every forty-eight to seventy-two hours. They insinuated that if a wife fails to provide this release regularly, it could cause her husband to fall into temptation. I bristle at the idea of using sex to keep my husband from looking elsewhere, but my best friend's husband had an affair two years ago and she's convinced that much of the reason was because their sex life had dropped off dramatically after the birth of their baby. Should I really just go through the motions to protect my marriage?

First off, I can't imagine what study suggests that men need sexual release every forty-eight to seventy-two hours, because that's absolutely not true. It may be that they were citing the amount of time necessary for a man's sperm count to return to full capacity following ejaculation (which is important if you're trying to become pregnant because your odds are better having relations every other day rather than every day), but it certainly doesn't

> **There is no set amount of time, physiological or biblical, during which a man *needs* to have sexual release.**

mean the man *has* to have release. The body will purge itself every few weeks by nocturnal emission (so-called wet dreams) if there is no other outlet.

There is no set amount of time, physiological or biblical, during which a man *needs* to have sexual release. However, the Bible does command us not to withhold ourselves from each other except to give ourselves to prayer and fasting.[1] We have emphasized several times that this verse can easily be misused, but we mustn't simply ignore it. God expects us to have fairly frequent sexual relations in marriage, and at least one of the reasons for this is because it helps decrease the temptation to look elsewhere. This does not mean that the withholding spouse would be directly responsible for the sin of his or her partner who goes outside of the marriage—we all answer to God alone. But there is a clear expectation that, just as sometimes the most loving thing is to abstain from sex when your spouse is clearly not interested or capable for some reason, there are other times when the most loving thing is to consent, even when you don't especially feel like it.

Consenting to lovemaking at these times should be different than just "going through the motions." Even though your libido may not be revved up, you can still be an active participant in *loving* your husband; don't dutifully give him your body while your heart and mind check out. Some of what he may need is the emotional connection with you that he finds easiest to make during lovemaking. When he gives himself to sexual enjoyment, you are seeing your husband at his most vulnerable and transparent. Remember our discussion of the importance of coming together in your child ego state. Meet him in that childlike spirit and you'll connect in a playful, intimate way that strengthens the marriage even if you weren't nearly as interested in sex as he was.

When my husband and I make love, it feels like it's always centered on him. He never touches my vaginal area, only my breasts. I feel uncomfortable asking him to touch me. It feels so selfish.

I'm glad to hear you're interested in having him touch you—you're trying to embrace more of your sexuality and celebrate the woman God created you to be. However, you will need to communicate that desire to your husband if this dynamic is going to change. Remember that we said lovemaking requires *mutual* exploration and giving as well as receiving. Your focus needs to be both on him and on yourself—this should shift back and forth, like a dance in which you trade who has the lead and who follows. The more this occurs, the more both of you will become aroused and the more united your spirits will be in *mutual* ecstasy.

If you decline attention or don't ask for it, you are actually encouraging selfishness in your husband. It's certainly not selfish of you to ask for mutual pleasuring! That's why God equipped you both to experience orgasms. Determine to tell your husband what kind of touch you'd like and ask for it whenever you make love. You'll both be more fulfilled as a result.

When I was with a group of women at work, the subject of sex came up. I was surprised at how many of them joked about faking orgasm—they said it keeps their husbands happy. I have never been able to achieve orgasm, but I've just accepted that. My husband wishes I could and I've considered faking it to make him feel like a better lover, but it just feels dishonest. Could it be a kind of white lie, done because I love him?

Absolutely not. Don't ever introduce dishonesty to your marital bed, even in the interest of pleasing your husband. There is only one thing Satan can claim to have created and that is lies; he's the father of them. There is no dishonesty, no deception in love. If you've been unable to achieve orgasm to this point, that's something for you and your husband to work on together, and the benefits of success will follow you all of the days of your marriage. Refuse to accept that it will never happen. Reread the sections in chapters 7 and 8 in which we discuss the key ingredients of orgasm in a woman. Experiment together and find out what's pleasurable. Read some of the books we recommend and begin doing the exercises they suggest. Work with a Christian sex therapist if necessary, but don't give up on this gift from God, and definitely don't begin to fake it.

I have struggled with my weight for years. It's difficult to look forward to sex when it centers so much on my body. How can I compete with the women with perfect bodies out there?

Don't try to compete. Your concern here probably has less to do with your actual weight and more to do with the culture in which we live. Western culture has a nearly impossible ideal for women's bodies—it's the thinnest 5 percent of a normal weight distribution. That means 95 percent of American women can't measure up to it! Many of those who do are plagued by anorexia and bulimia. This is certainly not the standard by which to measure yourself.

I love to encourage couples to study the paintings of women by the great masters. These were the idealized women of only a few hundred years ago, and they are very full figured. Many of them have fairly small breasts and much more normal-looking buttocks and thighs, some with obvious cellulite! They were definitely not hard bodies with 12 percent body fat and ripped abdominal muscles. Soft and shapely, with porcelain skin, rosy cheeks, and a healthy look in their eyes, they are quite a contrast to the models in *Sports Illustrated*'s swimsuit edition and much closer to the way God actually designed women.

This doesn't mean you shouldn't watch your weight or be concerned when you're overweight—we've already emphasized that your body is God's temple and we must always be about the work of temple maintenance. God is not glorified by undisciplined obesity. But if you are reasonably disciplined in your diet, get proper exercise and sleep, practice good stress management, and don't have some undiagnosed or untreated medical disorder, chances are pretty good that the weight you are at is the weight God designed for you. The challenge now becomes accepting your body and learning to cut loose and give yourself more fully to your husband.

> *All* women struggle with body image, whether they have a weight problem or not.

My friend and colleague Debra Taylor argues that *all* women struggle with body image, whether they have a weight problem or not. They complain that their breasts are too small or too large, their butt is too flat or too round, their tummy too big, their legs too short; there's always *something* that makes them feel self-conscious and reserved. To be sure, a husband who praises you is a big help in these struggles, but you can do a lot to address them yourself as well.

Remember that the most important sex organ we have is between our ears. Mentally rehearse giving yourself more completely to your husband—unabashedly, even aggressively. So much of arousal is

eroticism and seduction, embracing sensuality. These are not words we normally think of in connection with Christian women, but remember that we are talking about you and your husband in the privacy of your own lovemaking, and remember that we are claiming back sex from the enemy. He has perverted these words so that we think of them only in the context of loose women. *Claim them back for you and your husband.* Picture yourself teasing with your eyes as you slowly disrobe, your hips beginning to writhe. Light some candles and tell him he can look

> **Arousal has far less to do with an "ideal" body than with an absolute surrender to passion.**

but not touch as you unveil your secrets, eventually taking his hands and placing them where you want them. Few husbands can resist an assertive wife who is inviting him to enjoy her, confident in herself and her ability to please him. The arousal has far less to do with an "ideal" body than with an absolute surrender to passion. You'll both become more aroused by your seduction than you are inhibited by your body image.

Don't pass over the previous paragraph too quickly. Body image is one of the primary saboteurs of passionate lovemaking. There is no such thing as the perfect body, and many women develop problems with their bodies that are significant enough to prompt a total cessation of sex—if they allow their problems to become more important than they need to be. These might include lumpectomies or mastectomies from breast cancer, surgical scars from various procedures, severe burns, partial amputation or deformation of arms or legs from accidents, tubes or shunts protruding from the body to facilitate dialysis, colostomy bags or other medical apparatus, and numerous other physical problems. These are legitimate reasons to feel self-conscious, yet a couple mustn't allow them to take away the joy of frequently becoming one flesh.

Making love is three-dimensional—body, soul, and spirit. *Don't let your body rob the soul and spirit of your marriage.* As we said in the previous chapter, accept your reality, pray about it, talk about it as a couple, feel your feelings, grieve your losses, and move on.

Sometimes after my husband and I have a disagreement, he wants to make love. Many times the argument is still unresolved. The last thing I feel like doing is making love—I'm still frustrated with him! How can I make love in that spirit?

Some people would say that you can't and you shouldn't, but we are not of that opinion. Obviously it's best if the two of you can resolve the issue first before coming together. But if it's not a serious disagreement or a trust issue (like inappropriate behavior with women or money or the like), it may be an excellent time to make love, even if you can't seem to resolve the disagreement beforehand. Sometimes conflicts look different after making love. Remember that lovemaking is speaking your vows with your bodies. It's the ultimate body language. By coming together, you are saying, "For better or worse, I am committed to you. I love you. I receive all of you, shortcomings and all. Although we disagree on this issue, we are still one in spirit. I can strongly disagree with you and still love you with all of my heart."

In chapter 2 we cautioned that when a couple's marriage is characterized by strong anger, hatred, criticism, neglect, or disdain, the couple is unable to truly "make love" because their lives and their bodies send conflicting messages. Their sexual union would express a lie because they are *not* one in spirit and they do *not* really love each other.

When a couple simply disagrees on any number of life issues, however, they still love each other and are able to express it through lovemaking. If your marriage is an intimate union between two mature people, you can affirm your oneness through sexual relations even when you're not united on a particular issue. That issue may be easier to resolve after you're both reminded at the core of your being how much you love each other.

I am a home-schooling mom with four kids. Although I would love to celebrate my femininity and put more energy into my appearance, realistically I just don't have the time for it—or the money. My priority is raising the children. Are you suggesting that my priorities are off?

We certainly don't mean to be contentious, and, being home-schoolers ourselves, we are well aware of how difficult it can be to make time for self-care and to allot money for wardrobe, hair-styling, and the like. However, we argue strongly that much of child rearing depends on what is caught and not just what is taught. In addition to academics, character formation, spiritual growth, and social graces, one of the key things we want to shape in our children is proper respect and care for themselves, and that is largely caught through what they see in us. Good

> **Good self-care shows in our eyes and in our countenance, it glorifies God as we image him to the world, and it is extremely attractive to children who want to model it themselves.**

self-care shows in our eyes and in our countenance, it glorifies God as we image him to the world, and it is extremely attractive to children who want to model it themselves. We know of families in which these things were not modeled, and the girls (especially), who were not presented with a compelling picture of feminine beauty in motherhood, grew up rejecting not only the lifestyle of their mother but her family values as well. The self-neglect they saw in their mother was, understandably, not attractive to them.

Remember that one of the characteristics of the "wife of noble character" in Proverbs 31 is that she clothes herself and her household in fine linens, purple, and scarlet. Edith Schaeffer, wife of the great Christian philosopher Francis Schaeffer, poses the following challenge in her book *The Hidden Art of Homemaking:*

> Is it not important that a Christian represent in his clothing the One in whose image he is made? Spiritually, we are clothed in the white linen robes which are the righteousness of Christ, and that is more important than fashion. But is there any reason why a child of the One who designed, created, brought forth and *clothed* the flowers should set out to look ugly and drab? Are we representing Him by being unattractive?[2]

Rachel and I make a point of dressing up for our date nights. With all the other things screaming for our attention, this takes some real effort, and we sometimes feel a little silly when we go out to a restaurant and the guy at the next table is wearing a ball cap and T-shirt. But for us, this ritual of looking our best is part of the celebration of our love for each other.

Recently, as Rachel stood at the mirror ready to go except for finishing her hair, she mentally questioned whether or not all the effort was worth it. She had just concluded that yes, this was worth it because it was for *us,* when she noticed our six-year-old daughter, Grace, standing in the doorway with her mouth hanging open. No telling how long she'd been standing there, but she looked at Rachel in awe and said, "Mommy, you're so pretty it made my teeth drop!" At that moment, Rachel realized that it isn't just for us—it is also for *them.* Our children are drinking in a deep awareness of our love for each other, our care of God's temple, and our enjoyment of femininity and masculinity. This provides tremendous modeling for them in how to care for and celebrate their own budding femininity and masculinity. Make it a priority to practice good self-care—the benefits extend far beyond yourself.

My husband and I were watching a movie with a sexual scene that was pretty explicit. A few days later as we were becoming intimate, he wanted me to pose for him in a way that reminded me of the woman in that movie. I want to be a turn-on for my husband, but this just didn't feel right. It felt like he was more turned on by that woman than by me. Am I wrong to feel this way? After all, he's making love to me and not her.

It is never wrong to *feel* a certain way. The challenge is always to examine why you feel that way and to determine what to do in response to that feeling. In this case, your feelings seem entirely understandable because, in all likelihood, your husband did want you to act like that woman in the movie. This is an example of the concern we expressed in the last chapter about introducing steamy movies, sexually explicit passages from books, and fantasies about other people into your bedroom. It not only adulterates or contaminates the purity of what God wants the two of you to share, but it establishes some kind of standard that you begin trying to live up to, generally resulting in disconnecting from true intimacy and instead performing or playing roles for each other. As has been said, a wife can easily become living pornography for her husband by trying to be someone other than the full expression of who she really is. It's wonderful to experiment with variety in the ways you entice your husband, but don't try to model yourself after someone else and bring another person or an unhealthy standard into your lovemaking.

My husband occasionally asks to see my genital area. I am very uncomfortable with this. Honestly, it's an area I would rather hide than show off. It does not feel attractive. Do other women struggle with this or is there something wrong with me?

There's nothing wrong with you. Many women feel this way, and it makes sense. From the time little girls begin to experience vaginal secretions and become aware of the odors and irritation caused by even a little poor hygiene, they express frustration with "that part" of their body. Add in menstruation, urinary tract infections, messages about douches and sprays for freshness, the importance of ladies crossing their legs when seated, and biblical references to being ceremonially unclean, and it's no wonder this is not a part of the body most women are anxious to display. It seems a conflicting message to say this is a part that you save to give only to your husband; women might understandably plead, "Give me something else to give!" Many women actually psychologically block out this part of their body. They may enjoy and even flaunt their sexuality with their husband through their hair, makeup, jewelry, and clothes, and even through giving him their bared shoulders, breasts, legs, and behind, but they become entirely reserved and withdrawn in displaying their genitalia.

> **As a woman slowly alters her thoughts and feelings about this most private part of her body by seeing it through her husband's eyes, it can be wonderfully freeing.**

Remember that God designed the woman's genitalia and, like everything else he created, he pronounced it "very good." Most men are driven crazy by the thought of their wife opening herself up to him, and they love everything about her vulval area. A man's feelings about his wife's genitals are often quite different from her own, and it can be tremendously helpful for couples to discuss this. As a woman slowly alters her thoughts and feelings about this most private part of her body by seeing it through her husband's eyes, it can be wonderfully freeing.

To many men, this part of a woman's body is extremely alluring, mysterious, beautiful, and intoxicatingly powerful. Like the most exotic flower garden, it is a place to explore and become lost in. The Beloved in the Song of Songs seems to have understood this, as she croons, "My lover has gone down to his garden, to the beds of spices, to browse in the gardens and to gather lilies. I am my lover's and my lover is mine; he browses among the lilies" (Song 6:2–3).

Don't force yourself, but do try to become increasingly vulnerable with your husband in sharing every part of yourself, including your genitalia. Be sure to shower or bathe and perhaps use a perfume or after-bath splash so you won't be concerned about odor, but then talk and feel and risk and laugh, pushing ever closer to that place of being completely "naked and unashamed."

I am often so tired that sex is the last thing on my mind. How can we truly make love in the proper spirit when deep down I don't want to because I'm so tired?

This is one of the most frequent complaints I hear from women, and it is always at the top of surveys looking at women and sexual desire. Perhaps if men understood more about how critical feeling rested is for a woman's sex drive, they would help out more around the house so she could get some sleep. Fatigue is especially bad during the child-rearing years due to late nights with crying babies; nighttime feedings; the care of sick children; difficulty sleeping while pregnant; the energy drain of pregnancy, delivery, and breastfeeding; and the constant demands of little ones. Add to this cooking and cleaning, laundry, shopping, errand running, doctor visits, play groups, and other activities (often while balancing a part-time or full-time job), and it's no wonder that sleep can be much more appealing than sex.

Obviously an afternoon nap is a wonderful ideal, but it is usually not practical for working women and often not even for stay-at-home moms. Sometimes the best you can do is schedule lovemaking into the routines of your day or week so that at least it doesn't become last on your list and there is *never* energy for it. Consider making one night of the week a night when the kids have an earlier bedtime. Or plan Saturday mornings with things the kids can make themselves for breakfast and have them watch cartoons until you've had time together. Schedule Sunday afternoon "room time," with everyone in their bedroom for two hours reading or playing quietly or napping. Consider making love in the shower occasionally as you're getting ready for work.

Agree to a time limit on weeknights, say 10:30 P.M., beyond which lovemaking has to wait until the next day. The point is to acknowledge as a couple that rest is important for lovemaking, probably more so for the wife than the husband. Often men seem able to muster the energy even when they're dead on their feet. Testosterone is an amazing thing! Come up with some creative ways to integrate rest into your busy lives. Obviously you may also need to consider ways to slow life down a bit or get tested for possible medical problems if you are constantly fatigued. Exhaustion is a thief in the bedroom.

Many times when my husband and I are making love, I become triggered to a time when I was raped. I then begin to emotionally disengage and simply go on autopilot. How can I reclaim sex for the sake of our marriage?

It's good that you recognize what is happening and that you realize there is a need to reclaim something that has been taken from you and your husband. Based on the responses you are having, I would make the same recommendation I did in the previous chapter to the man asking about his wife's unresolved sexual abuse history. It's time to seek out a professional Christian therapist.

For some reason, in spite of the fact that nearly everyone acknowledges rape/sexual abuse as one of the most damaging things that can happen to a person, it is often difficult to convince people who have experienced it that they may need some therapy to work through it. Some of this hesitancy is probably a defense mechanism, looking for any excuse to avoid moving toward the emotional pain they know is lurking beneath the surface. Some of it is probably the shame of talking about what happened to them. Some may be the expense, although few people will let expense keep them from cancer treatment or other medical interventions. Some is probably pride, wanting to be strong and to believe they can work through their problems without someone else's help. Some of it may be disbelief that anything will ever really help the pain go away. Some may even be a belief that Christians should simply be able to "lay it at the foot of the cross" and be free from it without any further need to talk, grieve, or go through a process of healing and growth.

> **When damage occurs to our personhood through a relationship, our healing most often also comes through a relationship.**

Whatever the reasons for not seeking professional therapy for rape and/or sexual abuse, my advice remains the same: Get some help. When damage occurs to our personhood through a relationship, our healing most often also comes through a relationship. It's not that God couldn't heal it in an instant if he wanted to; he just seems most often to use others in the body to facilitate his healing. We are his hands and his feet, and it is no less a healing from God when it is mediated through one of his children. Seek out a trained Christian therapist and allow God to bring you the healing he has waiting. If you are unaware of Christian therapists in your area, you can check the Christian Care Network online through the American Association of Christian Counselors (www.aacc.net). For therapists certified through the American Board of Christian Sex Therapists, visit www.sexualwholeness.com.

Now that we're both in our late sixties, my husband and I are not sexual nearly as often as we used to be. I recently realized I had an unconscious belief that "old people" don't make love any more. I feel almost silly at times since we're obviously not spring chickens, but I don't want to lose that closeness. What is reasonable to expect in our later years?

Good for you for not wanting to lose that closeness! You've captured the heart of what lovemaking should be throughout one's life span. In general, the patterns a couple established earlier in their marriage will continue into their later years, and their enjoyment of each other will continue to deepen, just as the marriage should continue to deepen on every other plane. The intensity may not be what it once was, and there may be problems that were not experienced before, but these should merely provide a further opportunity to experience vulnerability as you work through obstacles together, rather than a cause for backing away when things don't work as they used to.

To be sure, there will be changes as our bodies age, arousal may be more difficult to achieve for both husband and wife, and orgasms may gradually become somewhat less frequent and less intense. As we have said, the man's erections will not be as firm and may be more difficult to maintain. Ejaculation may not occur with every sexual encounter, and he will likely require a longer period of time after ejaculation before he can have another. The wife will notice a decrease in vaginal lubrication during arousal and a thinning of the vaginal walls. This condition can be improved through the use of lubricants, topical creams, hormone replacement therapies, or other interventions recommended by your gynecologist. The vaginal muscles will weaken, but Kegel exercises will help greatly. (All women should begin doing Kegels somewhere in their thirties or forties. They consist simply of contracting and holding the pubococcygeal muscle for two to three seconds. This is the muscle that's used when stopping a flow of urine.)

> **The greatest problems encountered stem not from permanent disorders but from overreacting to the natural changes that occur with aging.**

As at any other age, medical problems and medications can greatly affect sexual functioning. Be sure to talk with your doctor if you notice changes. There are often alternative treatments that may not have the same negative side effects. In general, the greatest problems encountered stem not from permanent disorders but from overreacting to the natural changes that occur with aging. Worry and anxiety are your worst enemies in the bedroom. If things don't work as they once did, simply take it in stride, love and affirm each other, pray about it, talk with your doctor, and do some research, but don't panic. Chances are that your body is just slowing down, and there will be an ebb and flow to things that you once were able to count on without question. This is normal. If there are medical interventions that may help, pursue them under your doctor's advisement, but only after you've considered all of the above. Remember that the most important thing is for the two of you to connect at a deep level and celebrate your oneness in glory to the Father.

We love the playful yet powerful spirit of this poem written by a seventy-four-year-old woman and quoted in a book by Dr. Clifford and Joyce Penner.[3]

Finding the Fountain

The slim young man I married
Has slowly gone to pot;
With wrinkled face and graying pate,
Slender he is not!

And when I meet a mirror,
I find a haggard crone;
I can't believe the face I see
Can really be my own!

But when we seek our bed each night,
The wrinkles melt away:
Our flesh is firm, our kisses warm,
Our ardent hearts are gay!

The Fountain of Eternal Youth
Is not so far to find:
Two things you need—a double bed,
A spouse who's true and kind!

Just as we have said with so many other things that threaten the spirit of true lovemaking, don't let aging rob you of the joy of marital oneness. Enjoy each other as much as possible all the days of your life.

Questions for Couples

- What additional questions would you ask if given the opportunity right now?
- Are there any questions answered here that you need to discuss further as a couple?

- What actions do you need to take to address any of these issues?

- What do you feel is the number one female issue with sex in your marriage right now? What are you committed to doing about it?

12

Making Love
All Day Long

Husbands, love your wives, just as Christ loved the church and gave himself up for her.

Ephesians 5:25

The little chapel was nearly filled with couples for the marriage enrichment retreat. Rex and Monica, who spoke Friday night, had addressed healthy communication and set a wonderful tone for the weekend. Saturday morning's speakers, Mark and Kelly, were from the financial industry and had spoken on money matters. Mike and Livia addressed parenting Saturday afternoon, with everyone then being free until dinner.

It was now 7:30 P.M., and there was a sweet spirit in the air as couples laughed and chatted comfortably over dessert. The room slowly settled as Pastor Ted introduced John and Sharlene, who were to speak on sexuality. There was a subtle shift—a slight tension in the air—as they took the podium.

"Are you ready for this?" John asked with a grin.

Nervous laughter reinforced the anxiety he and Sharlene already felt. John pressed on. "Ten years ago, Sharlene and I were not even *remotely* ready for this. In fact, if you had told us we'd be up here today sharing what God has taught us about sexuality, we'd have either laughed or cried, depending on how acutely aware of our pain we were at the time. We were two hurtin' pups back then—two very broken people who somehow found each other and thought the other would be the answer to all of our pain.

"What we found instead was that when two hurting people turn to each other instead of to God, what they get is even more pain. It is only by the grace of God that our marriage held together as we eventually sought our healing from the Lord through a Christian counselor. And it is only by the power of God that we have something to share with you tonight about God's plan for sexuality in Christian marriage."

Sharing bits and pieces of the vision for sexual intimacy that we have detailed in this book, their talk went for an hour and a half. When it was over, several couples, some with tears in their eyes, shared how powerfully it had ministered to them. Two couples said they had been on the verge of a divorce before the weekend but that the vision John and Sharlene offered, and the witness of their marriage, had encouraged them to seek help instead. Many people said they had never heard such a beautiful affirmation of lovemaking in Christian marriage and that they had a different view of it now than they'd ever had before.

John and Sharlene scheduled a session with me after the weekend, just to process all that had happened through their sharing. It had been almost three years since we'd sat together in my office. Nine years earlier they had come in a last-ditch effort to save a marriage they both felt was already over. John had been into pornography and strip joints for years, and Sharlene had just broken off an affair. The very thing Satan had used to nearly tear them apart became the vehicle through which God brought their healing. Their journey to sexual wholeness is a mighty witness to the healing power of Christ and to the fact that God often uses the brokenness in our lives to do his greatest works in the lives of others. "My grace is sufficient for you, for my power is made perfect in weakness" (2 Cor. 12:9).

"It was incredible, Chris," Sharlene said. "I didn't know how we'd do, talking openly in front of all those people about sex, but the Lord allowed the growth that John and I have experienced to just flow out, and people caught more than just our words—they caught the spirit of what we were saying."

John jumped in, "You could feel the room relax as we kept talking. It's like, after they decided it was really okay for us to be talking about this, they dropped their guard, and you could tell they were so hungry for what we were saying! We could have easily gone on another hour and a half."

"Several people said it was their favorite part of the weekend," added Sharlene, "and not just because it was about sex. Actually, most of what we talked about was what you always said about the spirit of making love and making love all day long. Three different women told me in private that they'd always felt like sex was disconnected from the rest of their relationship and that now they saw the connection more."

"Guys talked to me in private too," said John. "I guess I used to think we were the only messed-up couple when it came to sex, but now I realize that a lot of couples struggle in this area. They may not have the same problems we did, but they still struggle, and a lot of times they don't know who to talk to. I couldn't help but think about what you used to say about Satan working in the darkness. All we did was start talking, and it's like people came out of the woodwork about sexual stuff.

"Pastor Ted said he hadn't realized how badly people needed to talk, and he's going to do a sermon series on it in April. He also said he'll talk with the board about possibly starting a support group for men struggling with sexual addiction. There's a pretty good chance it'll happen since we already have a support ministry for sexual abuse survivors and divorce recovery."

"And Pastor Ted's wife said she's going to bring a speaker in to talk to the women at MOPS about sexuality," added Sharlene. "Can you believe this? All from one little talk we weren't even sure we could give!"

I laughed and rejoiced with them. What a celebration it is when we realize God has brought us so far in our own healing that he is now using us to bring healing to others! But the truth is that I *could* believe the response they'd gotten from the retreat. It is the same response I get almost any time I speak on sexuality. The church and the world are hungry for God's plan for sex. We hope that by now you have caught the vision of that plan. Already you may be seeing it bring growth and healing to your marriage.

There are many ways in which we express love throughout the day in a healthy Christian marriage, and sexual love should always flow out

> **We are making, nurturing, growing, expressing, celebrating love throughout the day when we honor, serve, and cherish our spouse.**

of and be in line with them. This is why we speak of making love all day long. The Lovemaking Cycle is represented by a wheel that, once set in motion, should remain in motion, strengthening your marriage throughout all of your years together. We are making, nurturing, growing, expressing, celebrating love throughout the day when we honor, serve, and cherish our spouse. These behaviors create a spirit of love in the household (the mark of a true Christian[1]), and the giving and receiving of our bodies in sexual union then solidifies or seals that love; it reinforces and helps to perpetuate it.

A woman who heard me speak on this later shared how she and her husband had begun to tease each other when they were doing acts of service for the other. If the husband was changing the baby's diaper, he would laughingly say, "I'm making love to you right now, dear!" If the wife had cooked a nice dinner and set the table for a relaxing evening meal, she would whisper in his ear, "I'm making love to you!" What began as a little joke between them actually began to result in more frequent and more passionate sexual intimacy as they made these connections verbally throughout the day. The wife told me of coming home one day with groceries and noticing that her husband had fixed the wooden porch step that had always wobbled. As she mentally registered this small act of love on his part, she recognized being immediately desirous of him sexually. It was a breakthrough moment as she saw the pairing that had occurred between their expressions of love throughout the day and the sexual expression of their love.

> **Only love that has first expressed itself in a vow to love, honor, and cherish until death, *and then truly honors that vow,* can be confirmed through sexual love.**

This is a picture of making love all day long. Marital love is so much more than just a word or an emotion and so much more than just the sexual act; *it is commitment, action, devotion, and sacrifice.* If dating couples argue that sex before marriage is an expression of their love, we must counter that it expresses disobedience more loudly than love, because God has forbidden it. Only love that has first expressed itself in a vow to love, honor, and cherish until death, *and then truly honors that vow,* can be confirmed through sexual love. Only then can God be present in the exchange. All else is a lie, a mockery of truth, however passionately it may be expressed.

Importance of Our Actions

It's true that our actions speak louder than our words. Often men, especially, tell me they're not comfortable with physical displays of affection and that it's hard for them to say, "I love you." My advice is always the same: Do it anyway. So many wives complain that the only time their husband is attentive or touching them is when they want sex. By now you realize that this is the wrong spirit—it results in a *taking* and a *using* of the wife, rather than a *giving* and a *sharing* of their love. Spouses need frequent, tangible, nonsexual expressions of our love throughout the day if we want to truly make love sexually in the bedroom.

The world is drawn to a marriage characterized by a spirit of giving and sharing, though people may not know at first what power is drawing them. Children thrive within it, though they will not understand it until they are older. I had the privilege of growing up in a household in which my parents made love all day long. We kids soaked in the atmosphere of their "I love you's," their kitchen hugs, their acts of service to each other, and their cuddling on the couch. They dated each other, gave each other little gifts, and praised and thanked each other frequently. The greatest place in the world to be was squeezing my way into one of Daddy and Mommy's kitchen hugs, feeling enveloped in that tangible expression of their love. To be sure, Dad and Mom had their disagreements, but I don't ever recall hearing them yell—they honored each other. I remember Mom telling me when I was a teenager that she was so thankful she'd never had to question Dad's faithfulness. She knew she was cherished. I can't describe the security I felt growing up in that atmosphere.

Three Goals

As we said in the introduction, it is our prayer that this book accomplish at least three things. First, we pray that you, the reader, will gain a clearer perspective on God's great gift of sexuality and create more dialogue within the church, gradually helping to develop a far more comprehensive theology of sexuality; second, that you will wrestle through a greater ownership of your own sexuality, enabling you to experience a continually deepening sense of intimacy and connectedness with your spouse; and third, that this vision will inspire you to be more proactive in shaping the sexuality of the next generation, enabling them to finally launch a counteroffensive to the sexual revolution of the last century.

> **You can't *not* talk to your children about sex. You are "talking" to them every day in the way you interact with your spouse.**

Like John and Sharlene at the beginning of this chapter, many couples doubt that they could ever be used by God to positively impact someone else's sexuality. They feel they are too badly damaged; they're so messed up that God could never work through them. We urge you, if you have believed that, to reject that lie—nothing could be further from the truth. God uses broken vessels. If Satan has had some victory in your sexuality, do not allow him to have even more by keeping you from God's healing and robbing you of the joy of seeing your weakness used for God's glory.

Often couples believe they could never talk openly about sex. "I'd be too embarrassed. I can't even talk to my own kids about it!" Again, nothing could be further from the truth. You can't *not* talk to your children about sex. You are "talking" to them every day in the way you interact with your spouse. The question is, What message are you sending? As we said before, actions speak louder than words. Our life is our message. Our children, and those with whom we come in contact on a regular basis, will retain more of what is *caught* as they watch our lives than what is *taught* through our words. People are watching your life and your marriage.

Ask yourself what messages your children and others are learning from you about masculinity and femininity. What are they learning about caring for the body, God's holy temple? What are they learning about modesty, discernment, and discipline of the flesh, about celebrating and feasting, about proper displays of affection? Do people hear and see the language of your love in action? Are your children being nurtured within it? Is your marriage a witness to the beauty of sexual love within God's guidelines and to its bonding power?

God's Turf

We simply must reclaim sexuality as God's turf. Clarify what you believe and know why you believe it. Embrace a greater sexual intimacy in your bedroom and be willing to affirm it before others as God gives you opportunity. Hold to God's boundaries while celebrating his freedoms. Guard against its misuse while glorifying God through its proper use. Strike the balance with your children between preserving their innocence and preventing their ignorance. Continue to preach the message of what we are not to do, but couple it with the vision of what we *are* to do when two become one.

Questions for Couples

- ❧ Can you think of a couple you know who seems to make love all day long? What do they do differently than other couples?
- ❧ What specific things would you like to change so that your marriage could be characterized as making love all day long?
- ❧ In what ways has your vision of sexuality changed while reading this book?
- ❧ Are there people with whom you feel God is calling you to share this new vision?

Afterword

Rachel and I love to read classical literature. One evening after having completed the manuscript for this book, I was stunned by the following passage from Victor Hugo's masterpiece, *Les Miserables*. Hugo captured the beauty of heaven and earth meeting as a couple consummate their vows on their wedding night. He lifts the veil of the spiritual world to show us the angels and all heaven rejoicing as two souls are fused into one—it is the heart of the truths we have sought to convey.

> On the threshold of wedding nights stands an angel smiling, a finger to his lips.
>
> The soul falls into contemplation before this sanctuary, where the celebration of love is held.
>
> There must be glowing light about such houses. The joy they contain must escape in light through the stones of the walls and shine dimly into the darkness. It is impossible that this sacred festival of destiny should not send a celestial radiation to the infinite. Love is the sublime crucible in which is consummated the fusion of man and woman; the one being, the triple being, the final being—the human trinity springs from it. This birth of two souls into one must be an emotion for space. The love is priest; the apprehensive maiden submits. Something of this joy goes to God. Where really is marriage, that is to say where there is love, the ideal is mingled with it. A nuptial bed makes a halo in the darkness. Were it given to the eye

of flesh to perceive the fearful and enchanting sights of the superior life, it is likely that we should see the forms of night, the winged stranger, the blue travelers of the invisible, bending, a throng of shadowy heads, over the luminous house, pleased, blessing, showing to one another the sweetly startled maiden bride and wearing the reflection of the human felicity on their divine countenances. If, at that supreme hour, the wedded pair, bewildered with pleasure, and believing themselves alone, were to listen, they would hear in their room a rustling of confused wings. Perfect happiness implies the solidarity of the angels. That obscure little alcove has for its ceiling the whole heavens. When two mouths, made sacred by love, draw near each other to create, it is impossible that above that ineffable kiss there should not be a thrill in the immense mystery of the stars.[1]

Victor Hugo, *Les Miserables*

Notes

Chapter 1 A Crisis in Christian Sexuality

1. Genesis 1:28: God blessed them and said to them, "Be fruitful and increase in number; fill the earth and subdue it."

2. 1 Corinthians 7:5: Do not deprive each other except by mutual consent and for a time, so that you may devote yourselves to prayer. Then come together again so that Satan will not tempt you because of your lack of self-control.

3. Hebrews 13:4 (NKJV): Marriage is honorable among all, and the bed undefiled; but fornicators and adulterers God will judge.

4. 1 Corinthians 6:9–10: Do you not know that the wicked will not inherit the kingdom of God? Do not be deceived: Neither the sexually immoral nor idolaters nor adulterers nor male prostitutes nor homosexual offenders nor thieves nor the greedy nor drunkards nor slanderers nor swindlers will inherit the kingdom of God. Galatians 5:19–21: The acts of the sinful nature are obvious: sexual immorality, impurity and debauchery; idolatry and witchcraft; hatred, discord, jealousy, fits of rage, selfish ambition, dissensions, factions and envy; drunkenness, orgies, and the like. I warn you, as I did before, that those who live like this will not inherit the kingdom of God. See also Ephesians 5:3–5.

5. 1 Corinthians 6:18–20: Flee from sexual immorality. All other sins a man commits are outside his body, but he who sins sexually sins against his own body. Do you not know that your body is a temple of the Holy Spirit, who is in you, whom you have received from God? You are not your own; you were bought at a price. Therefore honor God with your body.

6. Romans 13:14 (NKJV): But put on the Lord Jesus Christ, and make no provision for the flesh, to fulfill its lusts.

7. Proverbs 5:15–19: Drink water from your own cistern, running water from your own well. Should your springs overflow in the streets, your streams of water in the public squares? Let them be yours alone, never to be shared with strangers. May your fountain be blessed, and may you rejoice in the wife of

your youth. A loving doe, a graceful deer—may her breasts satisfy you always, may you ever be captivated by her love.

8. Matthew 5:27–28: You have heard that it was said, "Do not commit adultery." But I tell you that anyone who looks at a woman lustfully has already committed adultery with her in his heart.

9. Judith A. Reisman and Edward W. Eichel, *Kinsey, Sex and Fraud: The Indoctrination of a People* (Lafayette, La.: Huntington House, 1990); Judith A. Reisman, *Kinsey: Crimes and Consequences* (Arlington, Va.: The Institute for Media Education, 1998); see also *The Children of Table 34: The True Story Behind Alfred Kinsey's Infamous Sex Research* (videotape documentary), produced by Family Research Council (Washington, D.C., 1994).

10. John Kippley, *Birth Control and the Marriage Covenant* (Collegeville, Minn.: Liturgical Press, 1976), 18.

11. Charles D. Provan, *The Bible and Birth Control* (Monongahela, Pa.: Zimmer Printing, 1989). This text lists ninety-nine Protestant theologians who taught against birth control and provides direct quotations from sixty-six of them.

12. John Francis Noll, *A Catechism on Birth Control,* 6th ed. (Huntington, Ind.: OSV Press, 1939), 11, 13, 30–34.

13. Theodore Roosevelt wrote, "The greatest of all curses is the curse of sterility, and the severest of all condemnations should be visited upon willful sterility. The first essential in any civilization is that the man and the woman should be the father and mother of healthy children so that the race will increase and not decrease." Ibid., 34.

14. See, for example, this brief quotation from a series of lectures given by Dr. Freud and recorded in *A General Introduction to Psycho-Analysis,* translated by Joan Riviere (New York: Liverwright, 1935), 115–16: "Perverted sexuality is nothing else but infantile sexuality, magnified and separated into its component parts. . . . Moreover, it is a characteristic common to all the perversions that in them reproduction as an aim is put aside. This is actually the criterion by which we judge whether a sexual activity is perverse—if it departs from reproduction in its aims and pursues the attainment of gratification independently."

15. *Griswold v. Connecticut* (1965).

16. Margaret Sanger, *The Pivot of Civilization* (New York: Brentano's, 1922), 271.

Chapter 2 The Difficulty of Talking Openly

1. Song of Songs 5:1: *(Lover)* I have come into my garden, my sister, my bride; I have gathered my myrrh with my spice. I have eaten my honeycomb

and my honey; I have drunk my wine and my milk. *(Friends)* Eat, O friends, and drink; drink your fill, O lovers.

2. Ecclesiastes 4:12: Though one may be overpowered, two can defend themselves. A cord of three strands is not quickly broken.

Chapter 3 The Spirit of the Act

1. Malachi 2:13–14: You flood the LORD's altar with tears. You weep and wail because he no longer pays attention to your offerings or accepts them with pleasure from your hands. You ask, "Why?" It is because the LORD is acting as the witness between you and the wife of your youth, because you have broken faith with her, though she is your partner, the wife of your *marriage covenant* [emphasis added].

2. John L. McKenzie, *Dictionary of the Bible* (New York: Collier Books, Macmillan, 1965), 154.

3. See Exodus 32:1–6.

4. See Numbers 25:1–3.

5. See 2 Chronicles 28:1–4; 33:1–6.

6. See 2 Kings 23:1–25.

7. Patrick Riley, *Civilizing Sex* (Scotland: T. and T. Clark, 2000), 106–8; William Smith, *Smith's Revised Bible Dictionary* (Zondervan, 1999), s.v. "Asherah" and "grove"; Robert Young, *Young's Analytical Concordance to the Bible* (Nashville: Thomas Nelson, 1980), s.v. "stones."

8. J. I. Packer, Merrill C. Tenney, and William White Jr., *Nelson's Illustrated Encyclopedia of Bible Facts* (Nashville: Thomas Nelson, 1995), 448; W. F. Albright, *Yaweh and the Gods of Canaan* (London: Athlone Press, 1968), 203.

9. Romans 2:28–29: A man is not a Jew if he is only one outwardly, nor is circumcision merely outward and physical. No, a man is a Jew if he is one inwardly; and circumcision is circumcision of the heart, by the Spirit, not by the written code.

10. The Council of Nicaea, A.D. 325, forbade the ordination of any man who had done so. (Cited in Rev. E. C. Messenger, *Two in One Flesh: The Mystery of Sex and Marriage, Part II.* Westminster, Md.: The Newman Press, 1950), 141.

11. If a boy began to get an erection, a row of tiny barbs around the penis would dig in, causing him to go flaccid.

12. Douglas Jones, "Worshiping with Body," *Naturally Healthy* (winter 2000), 8.

Chapter 4 Discovering God's Heart in Our Body

1. Romans 8:11: And if the Spirit of him who raised Jesus from the dead is living in you, he who raised Christ from the dead will also give life to your mortal bodies through his Spirit, who lives in you.

2. Genesis 1:31: God saw all that he had made, and it was very good.

3. 1 Corinthians 7:4: The wife's body does not belong to her alone but also to her husband. In the same way, the husband's body does not belong to him alone but also to his wife.

4. Genesis 1:26–27: God said, "Let us make man in our own image." . . . male and female he created them.

Chapter 7 Arousal

1. Song of Songs 2:16–17: My lover is mine and I am his; he browses among the lilies. Until the day breaks and the shadows flee, turn, my lover, and be like a gazelle or like a young stag on the rugged hills. Song of Songs 6:2–3: My lover has gone down to his garden, to the beds of spices, to browse in the gardens and to gather lilies. I am my lover's and my lover is mine; he browses among the lilies. Song of Songs 4:16: Awake, north wind, and come, south wind! Blow on my garden, that its fragrance may spread abroad. Let my lover come into his garden and taste its choice fruits.

Chapter 8 Apex

1. These are medical devices that draw blood into the spongy tissue of the penis, producing an erection sufficient for intercourse without the use of medications.

2. Archibald D. Hart, Catherine Hart Weber, and Debra L. Taylor, *Secrets of Eve: Understanding the Mystery of Female Sexuality* (Nashville: Word, 1998).

Chapter 10 Questions Men Ask

1. Proverbs 6:25–26: Do not lust in your heart after her beauty or let her captivate you with her eyes, for the prostitute reduces you to a loaf of bread, and the adulteress preys upon your very life. Matthew 5:28: But I tell you that anyone who looks at a woman lustfully has already committed adultery with her in his heart. Colossians 3:5: Put to death, therefore, whatever belongs to your earthly nature: sexual immorality, impurity, lust, evil desires and greed, which is idolatry.

2. Letter (March 6, 1956) from C. S. Lewis to a Mr. Masson, Wade Collection, Wheaton College, Wheaton, Illinois; cited in Leanne Payne, *The Broken Image* (Westchester, Ill.: Cornerstone Books, 1981), 91.

Chapter 11 Questions Women Ask

1. 1 Corinthians 7:5: Do not deprive each other except by mutual consent and for a time, so that you may devote yourselves to prayer. Then come together again so that Satan will not tempt you because of your lack of self-control.

2. Edith Schaeffer, *The Hidden Art of Homemaking: Creative Ideas for Enriching Everyday Life* (Wheaton, Ill.: Tyndale, 1971), 186.

3. Brecher, Edward M., and the editors of Consumers Reports Books. *Love, Sex, and Aging: A Consumers Union Report* (Boston: Little, Brown, and Company, 1984), 379.

Chapter 12 Making Love All Day Long

1. 1 John 4:16: God is love. Whoever lives in love lives in God, and God in him.

Afterword

1. Victor Hugo, *Les Miserables* (New York: Signet Classic, 1987), 1381.

Christopher McCluskey is a licensed psychotherapist, certified sex therapist, and certified life coach. He is a cofounder of the nonprofit teaching ministry Sexual Wholeness, which offers master's level training for Christian therapists and pastoral counselors through the Institute for Sexual Wholeness in Atlanta. He is also a cofounder of the American Board of Christian Sex Therapists. A nationally known speaker, Chris appears in the popular video training series *Marriage Works* and *Healthy Sexuality*, both produced by the American Association of Christian Counselors.

Rachel McCluskey, Chris's wife, is also a life coach and the homeschooling mother of their five children. She and Chris have coauthored several chapters in popular Christian books, including *The Complete Marriage Book, A Celebration of Sex,* and *The Complete Christian Parenting Book*. Rachel has done extensive research in the development of sexual theology as well as the historical and modern challenges influencing the diversity of views on sex present in the church today.

The McCluskeys live on a large family ranch in the foothills of the Ozark Mountains, alongside Chris's siblings, their spouses and children (sixteen so far!), his parents, and Grandma Gogey. They operate Coaching for Christian Living, an international life-coaching business, from their home on the property. They can be found on the web at www.christian-living.com.

OTHER RESOURCES AVAILABLE
ON HEALTHY SEXUALITY

Coaching Couples into Passionate Intimacy
God's Intention for Marital Sexual Union

A two-part live video presentation by Christopher McCluskey of the Lovemaking Cycle© and core material from *When Two Become One*. Ideal for use with adult Sunday school classes, marriage retreats, premarital counseling, marriage therapy, and private use.

(Run time 80 min.)

VHS $14.95
DVD $19.95

THE LOVEMAKING CYCLE

ATMOSPHERE
- Intimate Marriage
- Mature Lovers
- Privacy
- Energy
- Time
- Anticipation
- Initiation
- Mutual Consent

AROUSAL
- Playful Vulnerability
- Mutual Exploration
- Attention to the Senses
- Letting Passion Build

AFTERGLOW
- Restabilizing
- Cuddling and Caressing
- Affirmation
- Reflection and Basking
- Feedback

APEX
- Focus On Pleasure Building
- Greater Spiritual Connection
- Abandonment to Lovemaking
- Surrender of Control
- Climax

©1998 Christopher W. McCluskey, MSW
Copies available. E-mail request to: ChrisWMcC@aol.com

The Lovemaking Cycle©

High quality laminated posters of the model for use with counseling clients and small groups. Also available on as a Power Point presentation, developing the model i stages – excellent for large audiences.

8.5" x 11" Black & White	$ 9.95
11" x 14" Black & White	$14.95
8.5" x 11" Four Color	$ 9.95
11" x 14" Four Color	$14.95

(permission to photocopy posters for handouts is granted with purch

Power Point CD (24 slides) $19.95

Sexuality & Singles
Glorifying God with Your Body

A two-part audio presentation by Christopher McCluskey recorded live at John Brown University addressing adult singles and sexuality. Covers material from *When Two Become One* on a theology of sexuality and how to glorify God in dating relationships.

(Run time 60 min.)

Audio CD $14.95

*All resources available for purchase at **www.whentwobecomeone.net***